Study Guide

to accompany

The Psychology of Abnormality

by
Christopher Peterson
University of Michigan, Ann Arbor

Harcourt Brace College Publishers
Fort Worth Philadelphia San Diego New York Orlando Austin San Antonio
Toronto Montreal London Sydney Tokyo

ISBN: 0-15-503030-2

Copyright © 1996 by Harcourt Brace & Company

All rights reserved. No part of this publication may be reproduced or transmitted in any form or by any means, electronic or mechanical, including photocopy, recording, or any information storage and retrieval system, without permission in writing from the publisher.

Requests for permission to make copies of any part of the work should be mailed to: Permissions Department, Harcourt Brace & Company, 6277 Sea Harbor Drive, Orlando, Florida 32887-6777.

Address editorial correspondence to:
Harcourt Brace College Publishers
301 Commerce Street, Suite 3700
Fort Worth, TX 76102

Address orders to:
Harcourt Brace & Company
6277 Sea Harbor Drive
Orlando, FL 32887
1-800-782-4479 outside Florida
1-800-433-0001 inside Florida

PRINTED IN THE UNITED STATES OF AMERICA

5 6 7 8 9 0 1 2 3 4   095   9 8 7 6 5 4 3 2 1

Preface

This study guide has been created to help you understand the material in *The Psychology of Abnormality*. It is not intended as a substitute for the textbook, of course, but when read and studied in conjunction with the textbook, it should help reinforce your understanding of the concepts. The contents of this study guide are based on material I have made available to my own students when I teach abnormal psychology.

Introduction

The first section of each study guide chapter briefly describes the contents of the corresponding textbook chapter and proposes relevant learning objectives. I also alert you to the major concepts and to the important comparisons and contrasts between and among them. I suggest you read this section before you read the textbook chapter.

Chapter Summary

Each textbook chapter ends with a summary of the material covered, and this study guide section reinforces this summary by giving a somewhat different overview organized in terms of the major divisions of the chapter. Again, I suggest you read the study guide summary before you read the textbook chapter. After you have read the chapter in the textbook, return to the study guide chapter and work your way through it.

Glossary Terms

Psychology in general and abnormal psychology in particular can be misleadingly simple because the subject, after all, is us—fascinating and ostensibly familiar. But psychology differs from common sense because it is a scientific discipline, and like any such field, a great number of concepts must be mastered. The textbook identifies each important concept by putting it in **boldface** terms, and it is imperative that you grasp the specific meanings of these terms. These are not just vocabulary words but literally the material that comprises the field.

To help you learn these terms, I have listed in alphabetical order all the boldface terms from the chapter along with their definitions. I suggest that you be able to offer definitions—in your own words—for all these terms. Some students have found it useful to make flash cards for the most challenging of these terms, writing the term on one side of the card and its definition on the other.

Names and Dates

"Do we have to know all these names and dates?" Instructors differ in how they answer this question for their students, but I have offered my own opinion here by listing the names of the most important figures in each chapter. Your own instructor will tell you how specifically you need to locate each individual in history, but if nothing else, you should know the relative chronological order of these individuals, because each person's work invariably builds on that of others who preceded him or her.

Also, you should be able to locate individuals in their appropriate century, and if they fall within the 20th century, in their appropriate decade. You can do this most readily by thinking about what else was going on in the world when a given individual made his or her contribution to abnormal psychology. For example, Sigmund Freud's writing on psychoanalytic theory began during the Victorian era and lasted until the rise of Hitler. As stressed many times in *The Psychology of Abnormality*, ideas do not exist apart from their historical context.

CONNECTIONS TO OTHER CHAPTERS

The intent of this section is to integrate the textbook as much as possible, by pointing out how important ideas introduced in one chapter show up in others. So, depending on where the chapter happens to fall, this material may foreshadow subsequent chapters, review previous ones, or do both. Although the textbook necessarily breaks the subject matter into separate chapters, the field of abnormal psychology is coherent. To the degree that you can see its big picture, you are better served than if you master details in isolation from one another.

MULTIPLE-CHOICE QUESTIONS

One of the common ways of testing your understanding of abnormal psychology is with multiple-choice questions. In this section, I have provided the sorts of multiple-choice questions you will encounter in your course examinations. You will find that these are often quite specific and require you variously to remember names and dates, to compare and contrast concepts, and to integrate ideas or to apply them. Details matter.

Even if your instructor does not use multiple-choice questions, those I have provided should help you gauge how thoroughly you have grasped the material in the textbook. Correct answers follow the questions.

CRITICAL THINKING QUESTIONS AND RESEARCH PAPER TOPICS

Your instructor may raise thoughtful issues for discussion in class or may ask you to write about one or more of them. For each chapter, I suggest about 15 possibilities. If you are to write about one, in some cases, you might have to read ahead in the textbook to write your essay. In other cases, you might have to do library research. Remember that a good paper is one that takes an explicit stance that is sensibly supported. Please type your papers, and keep copies!

Some of these paper topics are similar to essay questions that instructors may prefer to use to test your understanding of abnormal psychology. You might practice for such tests by outlining possible answers, keeping in mind the specific concepts you wish to use.

FURTHER READINGS

Some of my students ask me to suggest articles and books they can read on given topics that particularly interest them. Although each textbook chapter contains references to the most important writings, there are usually hundreds of such references. I know you cannot look at all of them in a brief period of time. I have thus listed general and accessible readings by experts on respective topics, usually books but occasionally journal or magazine articles. The titles are self-explanatory. You should be able to locate these in your college library or local bookstore.

Christopher Peterson

Contents

Preface

1	What Is Abnormality?	1
2	Diagnosis and Assessment	11
3	Models of Abnormality: Explanations and Treatments	23
4	Research	37
5	The Case of Substance Abuse	45
6	Organic Disorders	57
7	Fear and Anxiety Disorders	67
8	Somatoform and Dissociative Disorders	77
9	Mood Disorders	87
10	Mind-Body Disorders	97
11	Sexual Disorders	107
12	Schizophrenic Disorders	119
13	Personality Disorders	129
14	Disorders of Childhood and Adolescence	139
15	Abnormality in a Community and Legal Context	149

CHAPTER 1

What Is Abnormality?

This first chapter introduces the subject of abnormality by considering first its definition and second how it has been conceptualized over the years. After reading this chapter, you should be able to do the following:

- Know why abnormality is difficult to define.
- Explain why abnormality lacks necessary and sufficient conditions.
- Appreciate that judgments of abnormality take place within a social context.
- Distinguish the three major historical perspectives on abnormality: the magical, the somatic, and the psychogenic.
- Know the important names and concepts associated with each of these major historical eras.

CHAPTER SUMMARY

Defining Abnormality

Any judgment of abnormality consists of a label placed on some action by a person and a recommendation, explicit or implicit, that an intervention be undertaken. Although judgments of abnormality are applied frequently in a wide range of situations, there is often disagreement about where to draw the line. Further, even when people's judgments are in agreement, the underlying rationales may differ from person to person.

Several operational definitions of abnormality can be found in the research literature: exposure to psychological or psychiatric treatment, diagnosis of abnormality, maladjustment, subjective definition, objective psychological tests, and the absence of mental health. Although each of these definitions captures part of what we mean by abnormality, none is perfect.

A precise definition of abnormality proves elusive because it is inherently a social judgment. Abnormality must be defined not simply in terms of what the "abnormal" person is doing but also by taking into account the perspective of the person making the judgment. As we currently use the term, abnormality is a fuzzy concept, in that it does not have necessary and sufficient conditions. Instead, it is captured by a family resemblance of pertinent—but not critical—attributes. Viewing abnormality as a fuzzy social judgment is not fully satisfactory, and thus we continue our attempts to characterize it more precisely.

The History of Abnormality

History reveals three major perspectives on abnormality. Magical explanations view abnormality in terms of the operation of evil forces. The somatic view explains abnormality in terms of bodily malfunction. The psychogenic view proposes that abnormality reflects a problem with a person's psychological makeup. These perspectives have each enjoyed a period of dominance, but all have been present for thousands of years, during which time they have intermingled. Regardless, each points to particular causes of abnormality as well as particular treatments.

"Magic" refers to a set of beliefs about the existence and operation of immaterial forces in the universe. Magical explanations of abnormality can be seen in the past, in such examples as trephination, shamanism, demonology, and witchcraft, as well as today.

Somatic explanations also occur throughout history, from humours to heroic medicine to general paresis. Today, attempts to explain abnormality in somatic terms are called the *medical model*. The medical model has been strongly criticized by Thomas Szasz, who brands the notion of mental "illness" a myth.

Psychogenic explanations of abnormality date back to Plato and Aristotle. In the 1700s, Mesmer popularized treatment techniques that we nowadays refer to as hypnotism. In the 1800s, the popular approach of mind cure legitimized to the general public a psychogenic view of abnormality. These psychological approaches often brought relief to people suffering from hysteria and other forms of abnormality.

The single most important figure in winning acceptance for the psychogenic view of abnormality was neurologist Sigmund Freud, whose psychoanalytic theory proposed that people's problems were due to unconscious conflicts. The neo-Freudians were theorists who followed Freud and extended even further his psychological emphasis.

Psychology itself became interested in abnormality through the efforts of behaviorists at the beginning of the 20th century. John Watson showed that "abnormality" could be produced by mundane processes of learning. Following from this view was the notion that principles of learning could be used to treat problems, an approach known as behavior therapy. Other psychological therapies that were developed in the 20th century target a person's thoughts and beliefs for change.

The history of hospital treatment parallels the general history of abnormality. Hospitals began as religious shrines; then they housed people who were not gainfully employed, including those with psychological abnormality. The mad were subjected to particularly harsh treatment under the assumption that this would help restore their power of reason. Around 1800, hospitals began to be reformed, and the insane were treated in a more humane fashion. It was at this time that physicians were put in charge of hospitals. Hospitals specializing in the treatment of the insane came into existence, and their directors were the very first psychiatrists. Clinical psychologists are now increasingly apt to work in hospitals, where they are demanding that psychiatrists share power.

GLOSSARY TERMS

behavior therapy—approach to therapy that uses principles of learning to treat problems in living

behaviorism—approach to psychology concerned with overt behavior and processes of learning

catharsis—the beneficial effects of speaking about long-repressed conflicts

cross-cultural psychopathology—the field that investigates problems in their cultural context

curanderas—individuals in Mexican-American communities who heal mental and physical distress

demonology—the assumption that people can be "taken over" by a spirit or deity, which causes them to act in unusual ways

existentialism—doctrine that a person's experience is primary

exorcism—procedure for inducing a demon to leave a body it has possessed

family resemblance—set of attributes that tend to cut across examples of a concept

free association—Freud's technique for unearthing unconscious conflicts; the person says whatever comes to mind without censorship

general paresis—progressive paralysis and loss of intellectual ability caused by untreated syphilis

germ theory—hypothesis that germs are necessary and sufficient causes of illness

heroic medicine—term used to describe medical practice during the 1700s and 1800s, when "heroic" interventions like bleeding and purging were routinely undertaken to cure disease

humanism—doctrine that the needs and values of human beings take precedence over material things

humoural theory—age-old account of illness that traces different diseases to imbalances among different bodily fluids, or humours

magic—special arts thought to liberate the immaterial forces of nature; magic includes certain words or spells, substances, and symbols

medical model—explanation of abnormality in terms of bodily injuries, illnesses, and/or defects

mesmerism—techniques for redistributing animal magnetism, known today as hypnotism

mind cure—a popular movement in the 1800s based on the premise that all human ills, including mental and physical distress, could be eradicated if people simply thought in the correct way

moral treatment—reforms occurring in the 1800s based on the idea that people with psychological abnormality should be treated in a moral and humane fashion

myth of mental illness—term popularized by Thomas Szasz, who argued that psychological abnormality is *not* an illness but instead a problem in living

neo-Freudians—theorists who follow Freud and are influenced by him, but who stress psychological and social determinants of behavior more than biological determinants

neurology—subfield of medicine concerned with diseases and disorders of the nervous system

operational definition—concrete measure of an abstract concept

phenomenology—description of an individual's conscious experience in terms that are meaningful for that individual

psychoanalysis—Freud's theory and therapy that stress the importance of unconscious conflicts in causing problems

shaman; witch doctor; medicine man—an individual sensitive to the immaterial forces found in nature and well versed in the arts of magic

trephination—Stone Age practice of drilling holes in the skull, perhaps to allow evil spirits to escape

witches—people, usually women, who supposedly make a pact with the devil and are thereby granted special powers

Names and Dates

American Psychiatric Association (founded 1844)
American Psychological Association (founded 1892)
Aristotle (ca. 384–322 B.C.)
Joseph Breuer (1842–1925)
Jean Charcot (1825–1893)
Dorothea Dix (1802–1887)
Sigmund Freud (1856–1939)
Galen (130–200)
Gheel (shrine established in 13th century)
Hippocrates (460–377 B.C.)
Hôpital Général (founded 1656)
Malleus Maleficarum (published 1486)
Franz Anton Mesmer (1734–1815)
New Age movement (contemporary)
Philippe Pinel (1745–1826)
Plato (427–347 BC)
Benjamin Rush (1745–1813)
Thomas Szasz (1920–)
William Tuke (1732–1819)
John Watson (1878–1958)

Know the approximate dates associated with the major events and figures in each of the three historical eras: magical, somatic, and psychogenic.

Connections to Other Chapters

The difficulty in defining abnormality surfaces throughout the textbook, especially in those chapters that discuss particular psychological problems (Chapters 5–14). The problems on focus tend to be good examples of abnormality, but the cautions raised in Chapter 1 remain.

The issue of continuity–discontinuity recurs as well. Subsequent chapters are for the most part arranged in order from those in which continuity seems quite obvious (e.g., substance abuse—Chapter 5; anxiety—Chapter 7; depression—Chapter 9) to those in which continuity is less obvious (e.g., schizophrenia—Chapter 12; autism—Chapter 14).

Finally, the social context of abnormality is another recurring theme. This refers not just to people's immediate relationships with friends and family members but also to their community, nation, culture, and historical era. Chapter 15 describes yet other aspects of abnormality's social context: the community and the legal system.

MULTIPLE-CHOICE QUESTIONS

1. Judgments of abnormality usually involve:
    A. a label placed on a person or behavior
    B. a recommendation for intervention
    C. both A and B
    D. either A or B
    E. neither A nor B

2. Defining abnormality in terms of "exposure to treatment" may fail chiefly because of:
    A. economic differences among people
    B. multicultural role demands
    C. the need for validation
    D. the problem of denial
    E. none of the above

3. Defining abnormality in terms of "maladjustment" may fail chiefly because of:
    A. economic differences among people
    B. multicultural role demands
    C. the need for validation
    D. the problem of denial
    E. none of the above

4. Defining abnormality in terms of "objective psychological tests" may fail chiefly because of:
    A. economic differences among people
    B. multicultural role demands
    C. the need for validation
    D. the problem of denial
    E. none of the above

5. According to the textbook, a judgment of abnormality is inherently:
    A. biological
    B. moral
    C. objective
    D. political
    E. social

6. Labeling theory is an approach to understanding:
    A. advertising
    B. deviance
    C. general paresis
    D. psychopathology research
    E. the insanity plea

7. According to the textbook, abnormality is characterized by:
   A. necessary conditions
   B. sufficient conditions
   C. both A and B
   D. either A or B
   E. neither A nor B

8. Ordinary language concepts are usually characterized by:
   A. family resemblances
   B. necessary conditions
   C. sufficient conditions
   D. both B and C
   E. none of the above

9. Operational definitions are always characterized by:
   A. family resemblances
   B. necessary conditions
   C. sufficient conditions
   D. both B and C
   E. none of the above

10. The textbook concludes that:
    A. a firm definition of abnormality cannot be proposed
    B. extreme examples of abnormality are easy to recognize
    C. there is an imprecise line between normality and abnormality
    D. all of the above
    E. none of the above

11. In all of the three historical eras, we see a concern with:
    A. explaining abnormality
    B. treating abnormality
    C. both A and B
    D. either A or B
    E. neither A nor B

12. The _____ era was the first to take dominant form.
    A. magical
    B. psychogenic
    C. somatic
    D. all of the above
    E. none of the above

13. The _____ era was the most recent to take dominant form.
    A. magical
    B. psychogenic
    C. somatic
    D. all of the above
    E. none of the above

14. Trephination is usually associated with the _____ era.
    A. magical
    B. psychogenic
    C. somatic
    D. all of the above
    E. none of the above

15. Shamanism is usually associated with the _____ era.
    A. magical
    B. psychogenic
    C. somatic
    D. all of the above
    E. none of the above

16. The *Malleus Maleficarum* is a manual describing how to:
    A. conduct scientific research
    B. prevent sexually transmitted diseases
    C. purify herbal remedies
    D. recognize witches
    E. treat anxiety disorders

17. According to the textbook, was "madness" ever distinguished from witchcraft during the Middle Ages?
    A. no
    B. yes

18. The textbook describes the New Age movement as mainly embodying a _____ perspective.
    A. magical
    B. psychogenic
    C. somatic
    D. all of the above
    E. none of the above

19. Humours are usually associated with the _____ era.
    A. magical
    B. psychogenic
    C. somatic
    D. all of the above
    E. none of the above

20. General paresis results from:
    A. childhood conflicts
    B. faulty learning
    C. genetics
    D. stress
    E. untreated syphilis

21. Heroic medicine lasted until the _____ century.
    A. 15th
    B. 16th
    C. 17th
    D. 18th
    E. 19th

22. In calling "mental illness" a myth, Thomas Szasz disagrees with ideas associated with the _____ era.
    A. magical
    B. psychogenic
    C. somatic
    D. all of the above
    E. none of the above

23. Franz Anton Mesmer was the first to develop techniques of:
    A. behavior therapy
    B. dream interpretation
    C. drug treatment of abnormality
    D. hypnotism
    E. psychosurgery

24. Sigmund Freud's original training was in:
    A. literature
    B. neurology
    C. psychiatry
    D. psychology
    E. theology

25. John Watson was the first:
    A. behaviorist
    B. *curandera*
    C. neurologist
    D. psychoanalyst
    E. psychotherapist

26. The first hospitals in Europe were founded by:
    A. HMOs
    B. local governments
    C. physicians
    D. psychologists
    E. religious groups

27. In most hospitals today, a _____ view prevails.
    A. magical
    B. psychogenic
    C. somatic
    D. all of the above
    E. none of the above

Answers to Multiple-Choice Questions

1. C
2. A
3. B
4. C
5. E
6. B
7. E
8. A
9. D
10. D
11. C
12. A
13. B
14. A
15. A
16. D
17. B
18. A
19. C
20. E
21. E
22. C
23. D
24. B
25. A
26. E
27. C

Critical Thinking Questions and Research Paper Topics

1. Consider several well-known examples of unusual people or behavior described in the media, for example, David Koresh, Michael Jackson, drive-by shootings. Which criteria of psychological abnormality does each exemplify? Discuss both research definitions and the pertinent attributes of abnormality's family resemblance.

2. Read a pop psychology book on addiction or fractured relationships. What conceptualization of abnormality is implicit in the book?

3. Would those labeled "witches" during the Middle Ages be considered psychologically abnormal today?

4. Compare and contrast the techniques described in Aristotle's *Rhetoric* for changing a person with psychotherapy.

5. Is abnormality a brain disease?

6. Suppose it were possible to conduct a genetic test that predicted subsequent abnormality. What ethical issues would result from the availability of such a test?

7. What are some contemporary examples of a magical approach to abnormality?

8. Many forms of abnormality are continuous with normality. However, can you describe any examples of abnormality that appear to be discontinuous; that is, those that do not exist in degrees?

9. What conceptualization of abnormality is contained in suggested health care reforms? (Pay particular attention to reimbursement procedures for prevention and treatment of psychological problems.)

10. Is there any link between genius and madness?

11. Visit a hospital and talk to psychiatrists, clinical psychologists, social workers, and other professionals who work with patients who have psychological problems. Ask these various professionals about their respective conceptualizations of abnormality. How do these fit together in the treatment of a given individual? What conflicts exist?

FURTHER READINGS

Andreasen, N. C. (1984). *The broken brain: The biological revolution in psychiatry.* New York: Harper & Row.

Boring, E. G. (1950). *A history of experimental psychology* (2nd ed.). New York: Appleton-Century-Crofts.

Brown, J. A. C. (1964). *Freud and the post-Freudians.* New York: Penguin.

Bursten, B. (1979). Psychiatry and the rhetoric of models. *American Journal of Psychiatry, 136,* 661–666.

Cantor, N., Smith, E. E., French, R. deS., & Mezzich, J. (1980). Psychiatric diagnosis as prototype categorization. *Journal of Abnormal Psychology, 89,* 181–193.

Ellenberger, H. F. (1970). *The discovery of the unconscious: The history and evolution of dynamic psychiatry.* New York: Basic Books.

Ferguson, M. (1980). *The Aquarian conspiracy: Personal and social transformation in the 1980s.* Los Angeles: Tarcher.

Foucault, M. (1965). *Madness and civilization: A history of insanity in the age of reason.* New York: Random House.

Frazer, J. G. (1922). *The golden bough: A study in magic and religion.* New York: Macmillan.

Gay, P. (1988). *Freud: A life for our time.* New York: Norton.

Hilgard, E. R. (1987). *Psychology in America: A historical survey.* San Diego: Harcourt Brace Jovanovich.

Marsella, A, J. (1988). Cross-cultural research on severe mental disorders: Issues and findings. *Acta Psychiatrica Scandinavica (Supplementum), 344,* 7–22.

Scott, W. A. (1958). Research definitions of mental health and mental illness. *Psychological Bulletin, 55,* 1–45.

Spanos, N. P. (1978). Witchcraft in histories of psychiatry: A critical analysis and an alternative conceptualization. *Psychological Bulletin, 85,* 417–439.

Szasz, T. S. (1961). *The myth of mental illness.* New York: Hoeber.

Watson, J. B., & Rayner, R. (1920). Conditioned emotional reactions. *Journal of Experimental Psychology, 3,* 1–14.

Weil, A. (1988). *Health and healing* (Rev. ed.). Boston: Houghton Mifflin.

Zilboorg, G., & Henry, G. W. (1941). *A history of medical psychology.* New York: Norton.

CHAPTER 2

Diagnosis and Assessment

This chapter discusses the related topics of diagnosis (placing people in categories according to their problems) and assessment (gathering specific information about a given person in order to make a diagnosis). After reading this chapter, you should be able to do the following:

- Describe the properties of an ideal diagnostic system.
- Know the history and details of the diagnostic system currently used in the United States: the American Psychiatric Association's DSM-IV (Diagnostic and Statistical Manual of Mental Disorders, fourth edition).
- Describe the five axes of DSM-IV.
- Specify the advantages and disadvantages of diagnosis.
- Explain how assessment allows the diagnostician to understand a problem's etiology, offer a treatment recommendation, and forecast its prognosis.
- Compare and contrast the different assessment traditions with respect to their assumptions about how best to recognize, explain, and treat psychological difficulties.
- Recognize the various tests and procedures that exemplify each assessment tradition.

CHAPTER SUMMARY

Introduction

Diagnosis refers to placing people in categories according to their problems. Assessment is the process of gathering specific information about a person in order to make a diagnosis.

Diagnosis

An ideal diagnostic scheme is one in which categories are mutually exclusive, jointly exhaustive, and defined by features that are either present or absent. No existing diagnostic system of abnormality is ideal.

Diagnostic systems have had a long history. One trend over the years has been toward increasing complexity. The founding father of modern diagnosis was the German physician Emil Kraepelin, whose distinctions among types of disorders provide the model for many of today's diagnostic systems.

During the 20th century, the American Psychiatric Association has published a series of *Diagnostic and Statistical Manuals* that have enjoyed widespread use in the United States for diagnosing abnormality. The current manual is the fourth edition, referred to as DSM-IV. It is notable because it attempts to describe symptoms in explicit fashion and to provide clear rules for making diagnoses.

DSM-IV describes people and their problems in five different domains called axes. Axis I describes clinical syndromes: acute problems that bring people into treatment. Axis II describes personality disorders. Axis III specifies pertinent physical illnesses or conditions. Axis IV notes problems in an individual's life like divorce or unemployment. Axis V requires a global judgment about how well or poorly the person is functioning.

Diagnosis is useful in part because it facilitates communication. Further, diagnoses may provide helpful information about the causes of problems, the treatments likely to help, and their probable consequences. Diagnosis is also problematic for several reasons, including the possibility of misdiagnosis, the doubtful assumption of discontinuity, the embodiment of the medical model, the questionable reliability of some diagnoses, and the stigma and self-fulfilling nature of labels imposed on people.

Although an improvement over its predecessors, DSM-IV can still be criticized on several grounds. There is no overall structure to the disorders it includes. The validity of many of its diagnostic categories has not been investigated. Furthermore, the reliability of some diagnoses is poor.

The future will see the continued development of diagnostic systems. They will most likely follow the historical trend toward greater complexity. These systems may classify problems not in terms of symptoms, but rather in terms of causes. We might also see some problems switched out of psychiatry and psychology into general medicine and other problems switched in.

Assessment

In the concrete activity of assessment, diagnosticians attempt to describe an individual's problem, understand its etiology, recommend a treatment, and forecast its prognosis. Diagnosticians have long searched for strong diagnostic tests, procedures that unambiguously identify the existence of particular problems. They have been unsuccessful so far.

Common to almost all assessment approaches is the diagnostic interview, in which the diagnostician gathers pertinent information from a client by talking to him or her. Part of a diagnostic interview is the mental status exam, a description of an individual's present psychological state. In recent years, we have seen a trend toward ever greater structure in diagnostic interviews.

Several different assessment traditions exist. Each takes a particular stance on the nature of people and their problems. Personological assessment regards people as complex and idiosyncratic. Here the diagnostician tries to describe people in rich detail, often preferring projective tests such as the Rorschach Inkblot Test and the Thematic Apperception Test. Psychometric assessment, in contrast, embodies a simple and quantitative view of people. In this tradition, the diagnostician tries to locate people along carefully defined dimensions by administering objective tests such as the Minnesota Multiphasic Personality Inventory (MMPI) or various measures of intelligence.

Behavioral assessment assumes that people are responsive to the rewards and punishments that prevail in the environment. Diagnosticians in this tradition describe what people actually do in particular circumstances. In cognitive assessment, the goal is to identify the thoughts and beliefs of individuals that create or maintain their problems.

Psychophysiological assessment encompasses a variety of procedures for measuring a person's bodily state. Often, the attention of diagnosticians in this tradition is drawn to indices of emotional response, like those measured by a polygraph. Neuropsychological assessment assumes that certain problems may stem from injuries, illnesses, or defects in an individual's nervous system. Tests such as the Bender Gestalt attempt to ascertain neurological abnormalities. Sometimes a wide array of neuropsychological tests is administered, such as the Halstead-Reitan Battery or the Luria-Nebraska Battery. Imaging techniques, such as CAT scans and PET scans, may also reveal neurological problems.

Family assessment starts with the premise that some problems are best regarded as interpersonal and thus need to be described in the context of the marriage or family.

GLOSSARY TERMS

assessment—process of gathering information about a given person in order to make a diagnosis

behavioral assessment—assessment tradition in which the diagnostician attempts to describe people and their problems in terms of actual behavior and the situations in which it occurs

Bender Gestalt Test—test developed by Lauretta Bender for measuring brain damage

CAT scan; computerized axial tomography—device for making three-dimensional X-ray pictures of the brain

clinical syndrome—an acute problem that brings a person into treatment

cognitive assessment—assessment tradition in which the diagnostician attempts to describe people and their problems in terms of the contents and styles of thinking that create or maintain difficulties

culture-bound syndrome—disorder occurring only within a specific culture

diagnosis—placing people in categories according to the problems they have

diagnostic interview—interview with an individual with the goal of diagnosing his or her problem

dimensional classification—description of people's problems along continuous dimensions, in "how much" terms rather than "either-or" terms

DSM-IV (*Diagnostic and Statistical Manual of Mental Disorders*, Fourth Edition)—diagnostic system published in 1994 by the American Psychiatric Association that is widely used in the United States

etiology—factors that have led up to a problem

family assessment—assessment tradition in which the diagnostician attempts to describe people and their problems in the context of their marriage or family

Halstead-Reitan Neuropsychological Battery—a well-known set of neuropsychological tests

intelligence quotient; IQ—the quotient of mental age to chronological age, divided by 100

International Classification of Diseases; **ICD**—World Health Organization's diagnostic system of medical and psychological problems

kappa—statistic used to measure the degree of agreement between diagnosticians, correcting for chance

Luria-Nebraska Neuropsychological Battery—a well-known set of neuropsychological tests

magnetic resonance imaging; MRI—imaging technique relying on magnetism to ascertain neurological structure and function

mental status exam—part of a diagnostic interview, in which the diagnostician attempts to guage an individual's present psychological state

Minnesota Multiphasic Personality Inventory; MMPI—a well-known personality inventory used to aid diagnosis

multiaxial classification—description of people and their problems in several simultaneous ways

neuropsychological assessment—assessment tradition in which the diagnostician attempts to describe people and their problems in terms of the brain and nervous system

neurotic disorder—problem marked by excessive anxiety, avoidance of problems rather than confrontation, and self-defeating tendencies; the person's ability to test reality is unimpaired

objective test—diagnostic procedure in which test scores are assigned according to explicit rules

personality disorder—pervasive style of dysfunctional behavior

personality inventory—a set of objective tests that attempts to measure the range of important individual differences

personological assessment—assessment tradition in which the diagnostician attempts to describe people and their problems in rich and complex ways

PET scan; positron emission tomography—device for revealing patterns of metabolic activity in the brain

polygraph—the so-called lie detector; a device for measuring emotional arousal

prognosis—the likely outcome of a problem

projective test—diagnostic procedure that asks clients to respond to ambiguous stimuli

psychometric assessment—assessment tradition in which the diagnostician attempts to describe people and their problems along carefully defined dimensions using standardized questionnaires

psychophysiological assessment—assessment tradition in which the diagnostician attempts to describe people and their problems in terms of physical systems

psychotic disorder—problem in which the person's ability to test reality is impaired

reliability (of a diagnostic system)—degree to which different diagnosticians arrive at the same diagnosis for an individual

research diagnostic criteria—explicit and unambiguous rules for assigning research subjects to particular diagnostic categories

Rorschach Inkblot Test—well-known projective test consisting of a series of symmetric inkblots

Stanford-Binet Intelligence Scale—well-known intelligence test based on Terman's translation of Alfred Binet's original test

strong diagnostic test—simple procedure that unambiguously identifies an individual as having or not having a certain problem

syndrome—pattern of symptoms presumably reflecting an underlying cause

Thematic Apperception Test; TAT—well-known projective test consisting of a series of ambiguous pictures

validity (of a diagnostic system)—degree to which a diagnostic system identifies coherent problems

Wechsler Adult Intelligence Scale; WAIS—well-known intelligence test for adults based on David Wechsler's original scale

Wechsler Intelligence Scale for Children; WISC—well-known intelligence test for children based on David Wechsler's original scale

Wechsler Preschool and Primary Scale of Intelligence; WPPSI—well-known intelligence test for extremely young children based on David Wechsler's original scale

NAMES AND DATES

Lauretta Bender (1897–1987)

Alfred Binet (1857–1911)

DSM-I (1952)

DSM-II (1968)

DSM-III (1980)

DSM-III-R (1987)

DSM-IV (1994)

Emil Kraepelin (1856–1926)

Henry Murray (1893–1988)

Hermann Rorschach (1884–1922)

David Rosenhan (1929–)

Thomas Sydenham (1624–1689)

David Wechsler (1896–1981)

In general, know the trends across history in diagnostic systems. And specifically, know the recent history of the DSM approach. Why was DSM-I created, and what led to each of its subsequent revisions?

CONNECTIONS TO OTHER CHAPTERS

Granted that the textbook is organized in terms of the major forms of abnormality (Chapters 5–14), issues of diagnosis and assessment continue to be important throughout. The conclusions offered about causes, treatments, and prognoses only apply if the problems are correctly identified in the first place. For the most part, the textbook describes problems in terms of DSM-IV criteria, although the criticisms raised about this particular system also figure in many discussions. Some of the psychological problems described in several chapters are quite difficult to diagnose with DSM-IV criteria in a reliable (e.g., Chapter 12) or valid (e.g., Chapter 13) manner. In other cases, problems that are not well covered by DSM-IV are discussed (e.g., Chapters 6 and 10). Chapter 14, which covers the problems of children and adolescents, echoes the point made in Chapter 2 that diagnosticians must be sensitive to the developmental stage of an individual.

The assessment traditions are theoretically based. Obvious links exist between these traditions and the dominant theoretical perspectives presented in Chapter 3. Similarly, there are links between approaches to assessment and to treatment.

Chapter 15 discusses abnormality and the legal system, which often interact in terms of judgments about a person's responsibility for a crime, his or her competence to refuse treatment, and so on. These judgments can only be made in terms of information gathered about the individual, and so assessment is highly relevant here as well.

MULTIPLE-CHOICE QUESTIONS

1. Across history, one obvious trend in diagnostic systems is toward:
    A. complexity
    B. coverage
    C. dimensional description
    D. etiological classification
    E. strong diagnostic tests

2. If a diagnostic system does not describe all possible problems, which property of an ideal system does it fail to possess?
   A. jointly exhaustive categories
   B. mutually exclusive categories
   C. present-absent defining features
   D. it fails to have any of the above
   E. it has all of the above

3. If a diagnostic system allows overlapping diagnoses, which property of an ideal system does it fail to possess?
   A. jointly exhaustive categories
   B. mutually exclusive categories
   C. present-absent defining features
   D. it fails to have any of the above
   E. it has all of the above

4. If a diagnostic system regards symptoms as falling along dimensions, which property of an ideal system does it fail to possess?
   A. jointly exhaustive categories
   B. mutually exclusive categories
   C. present-absent defining features
   D. it fails to have any of the above
   E. it has all of the above

5. The founding father of modern diagnosis was:
   A. Freud
   B. Hippocrates
   C. Kraepelin
   D. Pinel
   E. Spitzer

6. The diagnostic system currently used in the United States is a product of the:
   A. American Medical Association
   B. American Psychiatric Association
   C. American Psychological Association
   D. United States Department of Health and Human Services
   E. World Health Organization

7. The most recent version of DSM is:
   A. DSM-II
   B. DSM-III
   C. DSM-III-R
   D. DSM-IV
   E. DSM-IV-R

16 Chapter 2

8. In the current DSM system, clinical syndromes are described on Axis:
   A. I
   B. II
   C. III
   D. IV
   E. V

9. In the current DSM system, existing problems like unemployment or divorce are described on Axis:
   A. I
   B. II
   C. III
   D. IV
   E. V

10. According to the textbook, all of these are advantages of diagnosis *except:*
    A. assumption of discontinuity
    B. communication
    C. prognosis
    D. treatment recommendation
    E. all of these are advantages

11. According to the textbook, all of these are disadvantages of diagnosis *except:*
    A. assumption of discontinuity
    B. labeling
    C. embodiment of medical model
    D. treatment recommendation
    E. all of these are disadvantages

12. Concerning the future of diagnosis, the textbook concludes that:
    A. diagnosis will stay with us
    B. etiological classification will be undertaken
    C. systems will become more complex
    D. all of the above
    E. none of the above

13. At present, are there any strong diagnostic tests for psychological abnormality?
    A. no
    B. yes

14. A mental status exam is usually conducted in the context of:
    A. administering the Rorschach
    B. behavioral assessment
    C. a diagnostic interview
    D. psychophysiological assessment
    E. scoring the MMPI

15. Which assessment tradition attempts to gather rich information about the details of a given individual's life?
    A. behavioral
    B. cognitive
    C. family
    D. neuropsychological
    E. personological
    F. psychometric
    G. psychophysiological

16. Which assessment tradition attempts to describe people and their problems along carefully defined dimensions by using their responses to standardized questionnaires?
    A. behavioral
    B. cognitive
    C. family
    D. neuropsychological
    E. personological
    F. psychometric
    G. psychophysiological

17. Which assessment tradition attempts to describe what a person actually does in particular circumstances?
    A. behavioral
    B. cognitive
    C. family
    D. neuropsychological
    E. personological
    F. psychometric
    G. psychophysiological

18. Which assessment tradition attempts to ascertain a person's characteristic way of thinking about matters?
    A. behavioral
    B. cognitive
    C. family
    D. neuropsychological
    E. personological
    F. psychometric
    G. psychophysiological

19. Which assessment tradition attempts to assess a person's bodily state?
    A. behavioral
    B. cognitive
    C. family
    D. neuropsychological
    E. personological
    F. psychometric
    G. psychophysiological

20. Which assessment tradition provides strategies for identifying neurological abnormalities?
    A. behavioral
    B. cognitive
    C. family
    D. neuropsychological
    E. personological
    F. psychometric
    G. psychophysiological

21. Which assessment tradition attempts to describe people and their problems in interpersonal terms?
    A. behavioral
    B. cognitive
    C. family
    D. neuropsychological
    E. personological
    F. psychometric
    G. psychophysiological

22. The Rorschach would probably be used by someone favoring _____ assessment.
    A. behavioral
    B. cognitive
    C. family
    D. neuropsychological
    E. personological
    F. psychometric
    G. psychophysiological

23. The TAT would probably be used by someone favoring _____ assessment.
    A. behavioral
    B. cognitive
    C. family
    D. neuropsychological
    E. personological
    F. psychometric
    G. psychophysiological

24. The MMPI would probably be used by someone favoring _____ assessment.
    A. behavioral
    B. cognitive
    C. family
    D. neuropsychological
    E. personological
    F. psychometric
    G. psychophysiological

25. Thought monitoring would probably be used by someone favoring _____ assessment.
    A. behavioral
    B. cognitive
    C. family
    D. neuropsychological
    E. personological
    F. psychometric
    G. psychophysiological

26. A polygraph would probably be used by someone favoring _____ assessment.
    A. behavioral
    B. cognitive
    C. family
    D. neuropsychological
    E. personological
    F. psychometric
    G. psychophysiological

27. A device measuring genital arousal would probably be used by someone favoring _____ assessment.
    A. behavioral
    B. cognitive
    C. family
    D. neuropsychological
    E. personological
    F. psychometric
    G. psychophysiological

28. A CAT scan would probably be used by someone favoring _____ assessment.
    A. behavioral
    B. cognitive
    C. family
    D. neuropsychological
    E. personological
    F. psychometric
    G. psychophysiological

29. The Luria-Nebraska Battery would probably be used by someone favoring _____ assessment.
    A. behavioral
    B. cognitive
    C. family
    D. neuropsychological
    E. personological
    F. psychometric
    G. psychophysiological

20   Chapter 2

30. The FACES would probably be used by someone favoring _____ assessment.
    A. behavioral
    B. cognitive
    C. family
    D. neuropsychological
    E. personological
    F. psychometric
    G. psychophysiological

31. _____ is a syndrome found almost exclusively in the United States and Western Europe.
    A. Amok
    B. Bulimia
    C. Koro
    D. Latah
    E. all of the above

ANSWERS TO MULTIPLE-CHOICE QUESTIONS

1. A
2. A
3. B
4. C
5. C
6. B
7. D
8. A
9. D
10. A
11. D
12. D
13. A
14. C
15. E
16. F
17. A
18. B
19. G
20. D
21. C
22. E
23. E
24. F
25. B
26. G
27. G

28. D
29. D
30. C
31. B

Critical Thinking Questions and Research Paper Topics

1. What are the pros and cons of the DSM-IV approach to diagnosis?
2. In 1957, Timothy Leary wrote a book, *Interpersonal Diagnosis of Personality* (New York: Ronald Press), in which he sketched a strategy for describing people's personalities in terms of their styles of relating to others. Some have suggested that Leary's system can be generalized as well to the description of people's problems, which would result in a very different diagnostic system. Read Leary's book, and recast such familiar difficulties as substance abuse, anxiety, and depression in interpersonal terms. Critically evaluate your attempt.
3. What psychological problems are *not* covered by DSM-IV?
4. If dimensional classification is to be viable, the dimensions of interest must be specified. What are some likely candidates? (Hint: Consider the dimensions of "normal" personality specified by such theorists as Cattell, Eysenck, or Costa and McCrae.)
5. What are the pros and cons of each of the assessment traditions described in the textbook?
6. Is an integrated assessment strategy possible? (Hint: See Chapter 3's discussion of integrated theories.)
7. Talk to a mental health professional who specializes in diagnosis and assessment. What practical problems does he or she encounter?
8. Describe and evaluate how suggested health care reforms handle reimbursement for assessment of psychological difficulties.
9. What special issues must be addressed in the diagnosis and assessment of the problems of children?
10. What special issues must be addressed in the diagnosis and assessment of the problems of those from different cultures?
11. Are diagnosis and assessment biased by the race or gender of the individual being assessed?
12. The textbook discusses bulimia as a culture-bound syndrome of the contemporary United States and Western Europe. Are there other such problems limited to the here and now?

Further Readings

American Psychiatric Association. (1994). *Diagnostic and statistical manual of mental disorders* (4th ed.). Washington, DC: Author.

Carson, R. C. (1991). Dilemmas in the pathway of DSM-IV. *Journal of Abnormal Psychology, 100,* 302–307.

Gould, S. J. (1981). *The mismeasure of man*. New York: Norton.

Hodges, K. (1993). Structured interviews for assessing children. *Journal of Child Psychology and Psychiatry and Allied Disciplines, 34,* 49–68.

Korchin, S. J., & Schuldberg, D. (1981). The future of clinical assessment. *American Psychologist, 36,* 1147–1158.

Lebra, W. P. (Ed.). (1976). *Culture-bound syndromes, ethnopsychiatry, and alternative therapies*. Honolulu: University Press of Hawaii.

Lezak, M. D. (1983). *Neuropsychological assessment* (2nd ed.). New York: Oxford.

Lukoff, D., Lu, F., & Turner, R. (1992). Toward a more culturally sensitive DSM-IV: Psychoreligious and psychospiritual problems. *Journal of Nervous and Mental Disease, 180,* 673–682.

McCarthy, M. (1990). The thin ideal, depression, and eating disorders in women. *Behaviour Research and Therapy, 28,* 205–215.

Meehl, P. E. (1954). *Clinical versus statistical prediction.* Minneapolis: University of Minnesota Press.

Menninger, K. (1963). *The vital balance: The life process in mental health and illness.* New York: Viking.

Newmark, C. S. (Ed.). (1985). *Major psychological assessment instruments.* Boston: Allyn & Bacon.

Orlandi, M. A. (Ed.). (1992). *Cultural competence for evaluators.* Rockville, MD: U.S. Department of Health and Human Services.

Post, S. G. (1992). DSM-III-R and religion. *Social Science and Medicine, 35,* 81–90.

Rosenhan, D. L. (1973). On being sane in insane places. *Science, 179,* 250–258.

Schact, T., & Nathan, P. E. (1977). But is it good for psychology? Appraisal and status of the DSM-III. *American Psychologist, 32,* 1017–1025.

Simons, R. C., & Hughes, C. C. (Eds.). (1985). *The culture-bound syndromes: Folk illnesses of psychiatric and anthropological interest.* Dordrecht, Holland: Reidel.

Sochurek, H. (1987). Medicine's new vision. *National Geographic, 171,* 2–41.

Chapter 3

Models of Abnormality: Explanations and Treatments

This chapter discusses popular theories of abnormality. After reading this chapter, you should be able to do the following:

- Specify the sorts of questions that theories of abnormality try to answer.
- Define a scientific model.
- Compare and contrast the popular models of abnormality with respect to their assumptions concerning human nature, psychological health, psychopathology, and intervention.
- Know that no single model of abnormality suffices for all theoretical purposes.
- Describe attempts to go beyond the traditional models, specifically midrange (circumscribed) theories and integrated models.
- Compare and contrast primary, secondary, and tertiary prevention.

Chapter Summary

Models of Abnormality

Psychological theories of abnormality must address questions about risk factors and mechanisms. Theorists concerned with abnormality rely on scientific models: deliberately simplified accounts of human nature, problems, and treatment. Various models have been, and still are, popular.

Treatment

Various professions provide treatment to people with psychological problems. Clinical psychologists bring a psychological perspective to their work, and psychiatrists bring a medical perspective. Treatments can be roughly classified into biomedical therapies, which intervene biologically, and psychotherapies, which intervene psychologically. There is no such thing as generic treatment; all therapy is undertaken from a specific theoretical position.

Biomedical Model

The biomedical model assumes that people are physical systems. Problems result from bodily injury, illness, or defect. Treatment consists of biological interventions such as drugs or surgery.

Psychoanalytic Model

The psychoanalytic model assumes that people are energy systems. People have problems to the degree that their energy is tied up in unproductive defenses and symptoms. Psychoanalytic therapy aims at freeing this energy by bringing motives and conflicts into awareness.

Cognitive-Behavioral Model

The cognitive-behavioral model views people as information-processing systems, attempting to predict and understand events in the world in order to maximize pleasure and minimize pain. Proponents of this model see people's problems as learned and treatment as akin to education.

Humanistic-Existential-Phenomenological Models

Humanistic, existential, and phenomenological approaches take issue with scientific psychology's goal of specifying the causes of people's problems. Instead, these models emphasize the individual's conscious experience, ability to make free choices, and tendency to actualize his or her inner potential.

Family Systems Model

The family systems model assumes that individuals are inherently social and that their problems are manifestations of disturbances within the family. Therapy from this perspective aims at establishing healthier patterns of family interaction.

Sociocultural Model

The sociocultural model looks at people in terms of their larger society and culture. Problems result from stressful life events and lack of social support. Proponents of this view assume that these problems are best handled by undoing the social conditions that produced them in the first place.

Contemporary Explanations of Abnormality

Each individual model of abnormality fails to answer all the questions we wish to pose about abnormality. One response to this realization is to propose midrange theories, explanations that do not attempt to be broadly applicable. Another response is to search for perspectives that integrate insights of the traditional theories. An example is the diathesis-stress model, which explains abnormality in terms of preexisting states of the individual coupled with environmental events.

Prevention

Prevention of psychological problems is obviously preferable to treatment of problems once they develop. Nonetheless, there are barriers to effective prevention, not the least of which is knowing just how to go about it. Different strategies have nonetheless achieved some success. In primary prevention, the goal is to eliminate the basic causes of problems. In secondary prevention, the goal is to control problems before they become more serious. Finally, in tertiary prevention, the goal is to prevent the recurrence of problems.

GLOSSARY TERMS

analysand—recipient of psychoanalytic therapy

behavior therapy—therapy techniques based on principles of learning

biomedical model—approach to abnormality that assumes people are physical systems

biomedical therapy—treatment that intervenes biologically

biopsychosocial model—perspective on abnormality that acknowledges the role played by biological, psychological, and social factors

classical conditioning—process by which people learn to associate particular emotional reactions to previously neutral stimuli

client—recipient of psychotherapy

client-centered therapy—humanistic treatment devised by Carl Rogers

clinical psychologist—therapist with advanced training in psychology

cognitive-behavior therapy—approach to therapy that combines behavioral and cognitive techniques

cognitive-behavioral model—approach to abnormality that assumes people are information-processing systems

cognitive therapy—approach to therapy that targets for change a person's thoughts and beliefs

community psychology—application of psychological knowledge in community settings to prevent problems

couples therapy; marital therapy—treatment of a couple as a unit

crisis intervention—strategy of secondary prevention that helps people resolve life crises

defense mechanism—strategy deployed by the ego that protects the person from unpleasant realities

diathesis-stress model—model of abnormality that views problems as resulting from a preexisting state of the person (the diathesis) coupled with an environmental event (the stress)

eclectic therapist—therapist who subscribes to no specific approach to treatment but rather tries to take something useful from all treatments

ego—mental structure that takes into account external reality

ego psychologists—theorists who propose theories similar to Freud's but who place more emphasis on the ego as an active—not reactive—entity

existentialism—doctrine that a person's experience is primary, that existence precedes essence

family systems model—approach to abnormality that takes the position that all problems reflect disturbances in the family

family therapy—treatment of a family as a whole

feminist therapy—intervention informed by feminist philosophy

fixation—in psychoanalytic theory, failure to resolve a particular stage of psychosexual development, so that the concerns of that stage show up in adult personality

gestalt therapy—humanistic-existential treatment devised by Frederick (Fritz) Perls

group therapy—treatment of a group of people not related by blood or marriage

heritability—degree to which variation in behavior across people has a basis in variation in genes

humanism—doctrine that the needs and values of human beings take precedence over material things

id—mental structure containing irrational and emotional impulses

identified patient—according to the family systems approach, person who shows family problems most blatantly

incidence—rate of new cases of a disorder in a given period of time for a population

insight—bringing of conflicts and motives into awareness

mechanism—process by which risk factors translate into disorders

midrange theory—explanation of abnormality that does not attempt to be generally applicable

modeling—process by which people learn new behaviors by watching others perform them

neo-Freudians—theorists who propose theories similar to Freud's but who place less emphasis on purely biological factors and more emphasis on the social determinants of behavior

neurotransmitter—chemical secreted by one neuron that allows communication with other neurons

object relations—mental representations people have of themselves and others

operant conditioning—process by which people learn to associate responses with their consequences

overdetermined behavior—psychoanalytic assumption that even the most simple action has numerous causes

paradoxical intervention—family therapy technique in which the therapist communicates the message "don't change" in such a way that in resisting the intervention, the family indeed changes

patient—recipient of biomedical therapy

phenomenology—description of an individual's conscious experience in terms that are meaningful for that individual

prevalence—percentage of people in a population who have a disorder at a particular time

primary prevention—preventive intervention intended to eliminate the basic causes of problems

psychiatrist—therapist with training in medicine

psychoanalyst—therapist with training in a given field—say, clinical psychology or psychiatry—and additional education at a special institute that teaches psychoanalysis

psychoanalytic model—approach to abnormality proposed by Sigmund Freud that assumes people are energy systems

psychodynamic theories—group of theories proposed by those who followed Freud and were concerned with explaining the workings of the mind

psychosexual stages—according to Freud, stages through which children pass during development, defined by the part of the body that provides gratification of the sexual instinct

psychotherapy—treatment that intervenes psychologically

reciprocal determinism—Albert Bandura's idea that people and the environment mutually influence each other

reframing intervention—family therapy intervention in which the therapist encourages a more benign interpretation of what is going on in the family

risk factor—event or characteristic that makes a specific disorder more likely

schema—organized set of beliefs about some subject

scientific model—deliberately simplified version of some phenomenon created to facilitate scientific theorizing and research

secondary prevention; containment—preventive intervention intended to control problems before they become more serious

self-actualization—according to humanistic psychologists, inherent tendency of people to make the most of their potential

social support—supportive relationships with other people

sociocultural model—approach to abnormality that emphasizes the larger societal and cultural context in which abnormality occurs

superego—mental structure that has internalized society's dictates

tertiary prevention—preventive intervention intended to prevent relapse of problems

unconscious—according to Freud, mental activity kept from awareness because it is threatening

NAMES AND DATES

Alfred Adler (1870–1937)

Albert Bandura (1925–)

Aaron Beck (1921–)

Albert Ellis (1913–)

Erik Erikson (1902–1994)

Eros

Anna Freud (1895–1982)

Sigmund Freud (1856–1939)

Erich Fromm (1900–1980)

Karen Horney (1885–1952)

Carl Jung (1875–1961)

George Kelly (1905–1967)

Ronald Laing (1927–1989)

Abraham Maslow (1908–1970)

Frederick (Fritz) Perls (1893–1970)

Carl Rogers (1902–1987)

Harry Stack Sullivan (1892–1949)

Thanatos

John Watson (1878–1958)

Joseph Wolpe (1915–)

Know the chronology of psychoanalytic, psychodynamic, and object relations theories. Know when humanistic and existential approaches took form. Know when behavioral and cognitive theories began to be combined into a single cognitive-behavioral approach.

CONNECTIONS TO OTHER CHAPTERS

Obviously, what we mean by abnormality (Chapter 1), how we recognize it (Chapter 2), and what we learn from relevant research about intervention (Chapter 4) is relevant to how we explain it. As various disorders are discussed in Chapters 5 through 14, you will see that each model of abnormality can be quite useful for understanding some, but not all, problems. For example, psychoanalytic theory has a great deal to say about dissociative disorders (Chapter 8) but sheds little light on schizophrenia (Chapter 12). In many cases, integrated models seem to represent the most promising explanations (e.g., substance abuse—Chapter 5; depression—Chapter 9; schizophrenia—Chapter 12).

When we turn our attention to treatment, the dominant models of abnormality continue to be important, but the same caution applies. A particular model may provide an effective treatment for one disorder but not another (Chapters 5–14). Indeed, no single model provides all the treatment strategies we need. Perhaps an integrated intervention strategy would best serve those with the greatest number of psychological difficulties.

MULTIPLE-CHOICE QUESTIONS

1. _____ are associated with problems; _____ are the processes by which these translate themselves into problems.
   A. Causes; effects
   B. Effects; causes
   C. Mechanisms; risk factors
   D. Risk factors; mechanisms

2. Which of these is *not* a synonym for a scientific model?
   A. analogy
   B. metaphor
   C. replica
   D. theory

3. Models of abnormality make assumptions about:
   A. human nature
   B. intervention
   C. psychopathology
   D. all of the above
   E. none of the above

4. The textbook concludes that generalizing down the models of abnormality from adults to children is:
   A. an oversimplification
   B. never done
   C. reasonable only for less severe disorders
   D. reasonable only for more severe disorders
   E. usually a reasonable strategy

5. _____ are more likely to be depressed.
   A. Males
   B. Females
   C. both A and B; males and females are equally likely to be depressed

6. _____ are more likely to show antisocial behavior.
   A. Males
   B. Females
   C. both A and B; males and females are equally likely to show antisocial behavior

7. A concern with neurotransmitters marks the _____ model.
   A. biomedical
   B. cognitive-behavioral
   C. family systems
   D. humanistic-existential-phenomenological
   E. psychoanalytic
   F. sociocultural

8. A concern with heritability marks the _____ model.
   A. biomedical
   B. cognitive-behavioral
   C. family systems
   D. humanistic-existential-phenomenological
   E. psychoanalytic
   F. sociocultural

9. Most psychiatric drugs presumably work by affecting:
   A. brain structure
   B. neurotransmitters
   C. the endocrine system
   D. the immune system

10. A concern with overdetermined behavior marks the _____ model.
    A. biomedical
    B. cognitive-behavioral
    C. family systems
    D. humanistic-existential-phenomenological
    E. psychoanalytic
    F. sociocultural

11. A concern with defense mechanisms marks the _____ model.
    A. biomedical
    B. cognitive-behavioral
    C. family systems
    D. humanistic-existential-phenomenological
    E. psychoanalytic
    F. sociocultural

12. A concern with dream interpretation marks the _____ model.
    A. biomedical
    B. cognitive-behavioral
    C. family systems
    D. humanistic-existential-phenomenological
    E. psychoanalytic
    F. sociocultural

13. Psychodynamic therapists today usually agree with Freud's emphasis on:
    A. early experiences
    B. emotional conflicts
    C. the unconscious
    D. all of the above
    E. none of the above

14. A concern with classical conditioning marks the _____ model.
    A. biomedical
    B. cognitive-behavioral
    C. family systems
    D. humanistic-existential-phenomenological
    E. psychoanalytic
    F. sociocultural

15. One of the very first behavior therapies was:
    A. cognitive therapy
    B. dereflection
    C. parent training
    D. systematic desensitization
    E. thought stopping

16. _____ is (was) a cognitive therapist.
    A. Beck
    B. Ellis
    C. Kelly
    D. all of the above
    E. none of the above

17. A concern with conscious striving marks the _____ model.
    A. biomedical
    B. cognitive-behavioral
    C. family systems
    D. humanistic-existential-phenomenological
    E. psychoanalytic
    F. sociocultural

18. A concern with self-actualization marks the _____ model.
    A. biomedical
    B. cognitive-behavioral
    C. family systems
    D. humanistic-existential-phenomenological
    E. psychoanalytic
    F. sociocultural

19. Carl Rogers was a pioneer in _____ therapy.
    A. behavior
    B. client-centered
    C. family
    D. gestalt
    E. psychodynamic

20. Fritz Perls was a pioneer in _____ therapy.
    A. behavior
    B. client-centered
    C. family
    D. gestalt
    E. psychodynamic

21. A concern with SES marks the _____ model.
    A. biomedical
    B. cognitive-behavioral
    C. family systems
    D. humanistic-existential-phenomenological
    E. psychoanalytic
    F. sociocultural

22. A concern with social support marks the _____ model.
    A. biomedical
    B. cognitive-behavioral
    C. family systems
    D. humanistic-existential-phenomenological
    E. psychoanalytic
    F. sociocultural

23. A concern with socially prescribed roles marks the _____ model.
    A. biomedical
    B. cognitive-behavioral
    C. family systems
    D. humanistic-existential-phenomenological
    E. psychoanalytic
    F. sociocultural

24. Treatment from the _____ perspective emphasizes insight.
    A. biomedical
    B. cognitive-behavioral
    C. family systems
    D. humanistic-existential-phenomenological
    E. psychoanalytic
    F. sociocultural

25. Treatment from the _____ perspective emphasizes drugs.
    A. biomedical
    B. cognitive-behavioral
    C. family systems
    D. humanistic-existential-phenomenological
    E. psychoanalytic
    F. sociocultural

26. Treatment from the _____ perspective emphasizes learning.
    A. biomedical
    B. cognitive-behavioral
    C. family systems
    D. humanistic-existential-phenomenological
    E. psychoanalytic
    F. sociocultural

27. Treatment from the _____ perspective emphasizes authenticity.
    A. biomedical
    B. cognitive-behavioral
    C. family systems
    D. humanistic-existential-phenomenological
    E. psychoanalytic
    F. sociocultural

28. Treatment from the _____ perspective emphasizes prevention.
    A. biomedical
    B. cognitive-behavioral
    C. family systems
    D. humanistic-existential-phenomenological
    E. psychoanalytic
    F. sociocultural

29. _____ is (are) *not* an example of an integrated model.
    A. Midrange theories
    B. The biopsychosocial model
    C. The diathesis-stress model
    D. all of the above are examples
    E. none of the above is an example

30. In _____ prevention, the basic causes of problems are eliminated.
    A. primary
    B. secondary
    C. tertiary
    D. all of the above
    E. none of the above

31. Mental health education is an example of _____ prevention.
    A. primary
    B. secondary
    C. tertiary
    D. all of the above
    E. none of the above

32. In _____ prevention, problems are controlled before they become more serious.
    A. primary
    B. secondary
    C. tertiary
    D. all of the above
    E. none of the above

33. Self-help groups are an example of _____ prevention.
    A. primary
    B. secondary
    C. tertiary
    D. all of the above
    E. none of the above

34. In _____ prevention, relapse is prevented.
    A. primary
    B. secondary
    C. tertiary
    D. all of the above
    E. none of the above

35. Halfway houses are an example of _____ prevention.
    A. primary
    B. secondary
    C. tertiary
    D. all of the above
    E. none of the above

ANSWERS TO MULTIPLE-CHOICE QUESTIONS

1. D
2. C
3. D
4. A
5. B
6. A
7. A
8. A
9. B
10. E
11. E
12. E
13. D
14. B
15. D
16. D
17. D
18. D
19. B
20. D
21. F
22. F
23. F
24. E
25. A
26. B
27. D
28. F
29. A
30. A
31. A
32. B
33. B
34. C
35. C

CRITICAL THINKING QUESTIONS AND RESEARCH PAPER TOPICS

1. Is the textbook's distinction between biomedical therapies and psychotherapies a false one?

2. Are treatments that combine medication and psychotherapy usually most effective?

3. Might we want to call the recipients of treatment *customers* instead of *patients* or *clients*? (Hint: Learn about the origins of each of these words.)

4. What problems are treated with psychosurgery today?

5. Compare and contrast psychoanalysis and psychodynamic therapy.

6. For what problems do cognitive-behavioral strategies of treatment *not* work?

7. In what ways is Aaron Beck's cognitive therapy behavioral?

8. What are the pros and cons of each of the major theoretical perspectives on abnormality?

9. Provide examples of disorders well explained by each of the major theoretical perspectives.

10. Provide examples of disorders poorly explained by each of the major theoretical perspectives.

11. Describe how a given disorder, such as anxiety (Chapter 7), depression (Chapter 9), or schizophrenia (Chapter 12), might be explained in biopsychosocial terms.

12. Critique the integrative models described in the textbook.

13. Are there cultures around the world to which specific theories of abnormality seem to apply particularly well?

14. Evaluate the integrated treatments currently available for anxiety and depression.

15. Defend the use of a single model of abnormality by a therapist.

16. Can you match disorders with effective treatments? What generalizations can you offer from this exercise?

17. Critically evaluate feminist therapy. What do the relevant outcome studies show about its effects?

FURTHER READINGS

Albee, G. W. (1982). Preventing psychopathology and promoting human potential. *American Psychologist, 37,* 1043–1050.

Andreasen, N. C. (1984). *The broken brain: The biological revolution in psychiatry.* New York: Harper & Row.

Bandura, A. (1986). *Social foundations of thought and action.* Englewood Cliffs, NJ: Prentice-Hall.

Chodorow, N. (1989). *Feminism and psychoanalytic theory.* New Haven, CT: Yale University Press.

Cohen, S., & Syme, S. L. (1985). *Social support and health.* Orlando, FL: Academic Press.

Engel, G. L. (1980). The clinical application of the biopsychosocial model. *American Journal of Psychiatry, 137,* 535–544.

Enns, C. Z. (1993). Twenty years of feminist counseling and therapy: From naming biases to implementing multifaceted practice. *Counseling Psychologist, 21,* 3–87.

Fairweather, G. W., Sanders, D. H., Cressler, D. L., & Maynard, H. (1969). *Community life for the mentally ill.* Chicago: Alpine.

Freud, A. (1937). *The ego and the mechanisms of defense.* London: Hogarth.

Freud, S. (1900). The interpretation of dreams. *Standard edition* (Vol. 4). London: Hogarth.

Freud, S. (1916–1917). Introductory lectures on psychoanalysis. *Standard edition* (Vols. 15–16). London: Hogarth.

Freud, S. (1930). Civilization and its discontents. *Standard edition* (Vol. 21). London: Hogarth.

Garfield, S. L., & Bergin, A. E. (Eds.). (1986). *Handbook of psychotherapy and behavior change* (3rd ed.). New York: Wiley.

Greenberg, J. R., & Mitchell, S. A. (1983). *Object relations in psychoanalytic theory.* Cambridge: Harvard University Press.

Haley, J. (1987). *Problem-solving therapy* (2nd ed.). San Francisco: Jossey-Bass.

Haley, J. (1973). *Uncommon therapy: The psychiatric techniques of Milton H. Erickson, M.D.* New York: Norton.

Laing, R. D. (1959). *The divided self.* London: Tavistok.

Lindemann, E. (1944). Symptomatology and management of acute grief. *American Journal of Psychiatry, 101,* 141–148.

Luborsky, L. (1984). *Principles of psychoanalytic psychotherapy.* New York: Basic Books.

Mahoney, M. J. (1974). *Cognition and behavior modification.* Cambridge: Ballinger.

Maslow, A. H. (1966). *The psychology of science: A reconnaissance.* New York: Harper & Row.

May, R. (1969). *Existential psychology* (2nd ed.). New York: Random House.

Meichenbaum, D. (1977). *Cognitive behavior-modification: An integrative approach.* New York: Plenum.

Minuchin, S. (1974). *Families and family therapy.* Cambridge: Harvard University Press.

Monroe, S. M., & Simons, A. D. (1991). Diathesis-stress theories in the context of life stress research: Implications for the depressive disorders. *Psychological Bulletin, 110,* 406–425.

Munoz, R. F., Snowden, L. R., & Kelly, J. G. (Eds.). (1979). *Social and psychological research in community settings.* San Francisco: Jossey-Bass.

Perls, F. S. (1969). *Gestalt therapy verbatim.* Lafayette, CA: Real People Press.

Rogers, C. R. (1951). *Client-centered therapy: Its current practice, implications, and theory.* Boston: Houghton Mifflin.

Rogers, C. R. (1961). *On becoming a person.* Boston: Houghton Mifflin.

Strupp, H. H., Hadley, S. W., & Gomes-Schwartz, B. (1977). *Psychotherapy for better or worse: An analysis of the problem of negative effects.* New York: Jason Aronson.

Tomkins, C. (1976, January 5). New paradigms. *New Yorker,* 30–36+.

Vaillant, G. E. (1977). *Adaptation to life.* Boston: Little, Brown.

Wolpe, J. (1958). *Psychotherapy by reciprocal inhibition.* Stanford CA: Stanford University Press.

Wortman, C. B., & Silver, R. C. (1989). The myths of coping with loss. *Journal of Consulting and Clinical Psychology, 57,* 349–357.

Yalom, I. D. (1985). *The theory and practice of group psychotherapy* (3rd ed.). New York: Basic Books.

CHAPTER 4

Research

This chapter discusses research methods and how the effectiveness of psychotherapy has been investigated. After reading this chapter, you should be able to do the following:

- Describe the general concerns of all researchers.
- Compare and contrast different research strategies—case studies, correlational investigations, and experiments—in terms of their strengths and weaknesses.
- Know that an investigator chooses a particular research strategy based on his or her purposes.
- Describe the history of attempts to demonstrate the effectiveness of psychotherapy.
- Understand why these attempts finally were fruitful.

CHAPTER SUMMARY

Methods

All researchers are concerned with several general issues. One of these is how representative their sample is of the more general population to which they wish their conclusions to apply. Another basic issue is how to offer sound conclusions about the samples actually studied. Findings that are statistically significant are given the most emphasis, but researchers must still judge the practical significance of these results. Another basic decision an investigator must make concerns the type of abnormality to be studied and the way it is to be measured. Research design refers to the overall structure of a study. The goal is a research design that allows conclusions about the question of interest and minimizes alternative interpretations.

Several research strategies for studying abnormality exist, each with characteristic strengths and weaknesses. Case studies provide rich details but have problems with fidelity of information, generalization of conclusions, and identification of causes. Correlational investigations lead to general conclusions but do not allow causes to be specified with certainty. With experiments, a researcher can identify operative causes, but this strategy can sometimes prove unwieldy or unethical.

Does Psychotherapy Work?

The effectiveness of treatment has long been unclear. Psychotherapy in particular has proven difficult to evaluate. The very first psychotherapy was psychoanalysis. It seemed effective when used with certain hysterical patients. However, as psychoanalysis began to be applied to other problems, its effectiveness was questioned.

In 1952, Hans Eysenck leveled the charge that psychoanalytic treatment did not work. Indeed, he argued that it was worse than no treatment at all. Although Eysenck's criticisms were not well supported by the research he cited, they were nonetheless influential. For years, it was believed that psychotherapy did not help people with problems.

The development of behavioral and cognitive therapies, coupled with greater sophistication about how to evaluate therapy effectiveness, led to a renewed interest in psychotherapy outcome research. In 1977, Mary Smith and Gene Glass reviewed the relevant literature and concluded that psychotherapy was, in fact, effective. They found no evidence that any given approach to psychotherapy was, in general, superior to any other.

Current research into psychotherapy effectiveness attempts to match effective treatments with given problems, identify critical ingredients in psychotherapy, identify common factors to all successful forms of treatment, study the process of psychotherapy, and investigate long-term outcomes.

Glossary Terms

analogue research—investigation of abnormality in the laboratory by creating phenomena analogous to disorders
case study—intensive investigation of a single individual
confound—an unmeasured variable responsible for the apparent relationship between two other variables
correlation coefficient—quantitative measure of the degree to which two variables show a linear relationship
correlational investigation—study of the relationship between two variables in a sample of research subjects
double-blind design—research design in which participants—both patients and therapists—are kept in the dark as to who is given a placebo and who is given the experimental treatment
experiment—investigation in which certain events are deliberately manipulated and the effects of these manipulations on other events are measured
experimental psychopathology—investigation of abnormality through experimentation
helping alliance—relationship between the therapist and client in which they see each other as working toward the same goal
longitudinal design—study that follows research participants over time
matching model—specification of which therapy works best for which problem
meta-analysis—statistical technique that combines quantitatively the results of separate experimental studies
multiple regression—correlational procedure that ascertains the associations between a set of variables and another variable in a sample of research subjects
nonspecific factor—ingredient in successful therapy that characterizes no given approach to therapy
operational definition—concrete measure of an abstract concept
Ortgeist—intellectual spirit of a particular culture
outcome research—investigation of the effectiveness of treatment
placebo effect—benefit due to expectations on the part of the therapist and/or the person with the problem
population—the larger group to which the results of a research investigation are intended to apply
real relationship—aspects of client-therapist interaction that reflect the facts of their practical existence in the real world
reliability—degree to which an operationalization yields the same results on different occasions
research design—overall structure of a research investigation and its elements
research diagnostic criteria—explicit and unambiguous rules for assigning research subjects to particular diagnostic categories
sample—the individuals actually studied in a research investigation
spontaneous recovery; spontaneous remission—improvement without professional intervention
statistical significance—inference whether results of a research investigation are due to chance
therapy manual—an explicit description of what a therapist should do in particular sessions
validity—degree to which an operationalization captures the concept it purports to measure
Zeitgeist—intellectual spirit of a particular historical era

Names and Dates

Hans Eysenck (1916–)

Know the history of attempts to show that psychotherapy is effective.

Connections to Other Chapters

All of the research strategies discussed in Chapter 4 are exemplified throughout the rest of the book. For example, case studies figure prominently in the discussion of organic disorders (Chapter 6), dissociative disorders (Chapter 8), and certain sexual disorders (Chapter 11). Correlational investigations are ubiquitous, for instance, any time sex differences or social conditions are linked to the prevalence or severity of a disorder. Experimental analogues are mentioned in Chapter 7 on anxiety, Chapter 9 on depression, and elsewhere.

Whether psychotherapy is effective is obviously of concern to those professionals who treat disorders by psychological means (Chapters 5-14).

Multiple-Choice Questions

1. Sample is to population as:
    A. correlational investigation is to experiment
    B. few is to many
    C. statistical significance is to practical significance
    D. validity is to reliability

2. _____ samples are commonly used in psychopathology research.
    A. Case
    B. Convenience
    C. Random
    D. Stratified
    E. Uncorrelated

3. The conventional level of statistical significance is:
    A. .10
    B. .05
    C. .01
    D. .001
    E. .0001

4. An operational definition specifies a(n):
    A. concrete measure
    B. integrative construct
    C. likely confound
    D. semantic critique
    E. significance level

5. The notable strength of a case study is:
    A. allowing generalization to other people
    B. identifying causes
    C. providing rich detail
    D. all of the above
    E. none of the above

6. The notable strength of a correlational investigation is:
   A. allowing generalization to other people
   B. identifying causes
   C. providing rich detail
   D. all of the above
   E. none of the above

7. The notable strength of an experiment is:
   A. allowing generalization to other people
   B. identifying causes
   C. providing rich detail
   D. all of the above
   E. none of the above

8. Freud favored the use of:
   A. case studies
   B. correlational investigations
   C. experiments
   D. all of the above
   E. none of the above

9. Sex differences are best studied with:
   A. case studies
   B. correlational investigations
   C. experiments
   D. all of the above
   E. none of the above

10. As described in the textbook, analogue studies are often:
    A. case studies
    B. correlational investigations
    C. experiments
    D. all of the above
    E. none of the above

11. The first psychotherapy was:
    A. client-centered therapy
    B. cognitive therapy
    C. psychoanalysis
    D. psychodynamic therapy
    E. rational-emotive therapy

12. In 1952, Hans Eysenck concluded that psychotherapy was:
    A. effective
    B. ineffective
    C. less effective than no treatment at all

13. A placebo effect is an obvious problem for arguing that _____ therapies are effective.
    A. biomedical
    B. psychological
    C. both A and B
    D. neither A nor B

14. Double-blind designs are most sensible for investigating the effectiveness of:
    A. behavior modification
    B. client-centered therapy
    C. cognitive therapy
    D. drugs
    E. psychoanalysis

15. Which is a historical trend that makes it possible to investigate the effectiveness of psychotherapy?
    A. objective measures of improvement
    B. popularity of behavioral and cognitive therapies
    C. time limits on therapy
    D. all of the above
    E. none of the above

16. A therapy manual is a(n):
    A. collection of objective measures of improvement
    B. diagnostic manual prepared by clinical psychologists
    C. directory of affordable services
    D. explicit description of how to do therapy
    E. history of psychotherapy

17. Smith and Glass concluded that:
    A. psychotherapy is effective
    B. no type of psychotherapy is more effective than any other
    C. both A and B
    D. neither A nor B

18. Meta-analysis is a:
    A. radical critique of psychotherapy
    B. specification of effective treatments for given problems
    C. statistical technique
    D. therapy technique pioneered by Freud's analyst

19. In matching models, what are matched?
    A. client income and therapist fees
    B. clients and therapists
    C. inner perceptions and outer reality
    D. minds and bodies
    E. problems and treatments

20. _____ is by definition unconscious.
    A. The helping alliance
    B. The real relationship
    C. Transference
    D. all of the above
    E. none of the above

21. Zeitgeist refers to the spirit of a particular:
    A. culture
    B. historical era
    C. religion
    D. research strategy
    E. scientific model

22. Ortgeist refers to the spirit of a particular:
    A. culture
    B. historical era
    C. religion
    D. research strategy
    E. scientific model

ANSWERS TO MULTIPLE-CHOICE QUESTIONS

1. B
2. B
3. B
4. A
5. C
6. A
7. B
8. A
9. B
10. C
11. C
12. C
13. A
14. D
15. D
16. D
17. C
18. C
19. E
20. C
21. B
22. A

CRITICAL THINKING QUESTIONS AND RESEARCH PAPER TOPICS

1. Find examples from the research literature that exemplify the different research strategies. (Hint: Look at recent issues of *Journal of Abnormal Psychology, Journal of Consulting and Clinical Psychology, American Journal of Psychiatry,* and/or *Archives of General Psychiatry.*) What are the strengths and weaknesses of each study?
2. Read a pop psychology book. How is research evidence used (or not used) to support its conclusions?
3. Trace changes over the past few decades in federal funding priorities for mental health research.
4. How does the effectiveness of psychotherapy compare with the effectiveness of such familiar medical treatments as antibiotics for pneumonia?
5. Will different psychotherapies eventually be distinguished by how well they prevent the recurrence of problems? By this criterion, which therapy seems most promising?
6. Support or criticize the following statement: Psychotherapy is effective only because of common factors.

FURTHER READINGS

Eysenck, H. J. (1952). The effects of psychotherapy: An evaluation. *Journal of Consulting Psychology, 16,* 319–324.
Frank, J. D. (1974). *Persuasion and healing* (Rev. ed.). New York: Schocken Books.
Maser, J. D., & Seligman, M. E. P. (Eds.). (1977). *Psychopathology: Experimental models.* San Francisco: Freeman.
Schachter, S. (1982). Recidivism and self-cure of smoking and obesity. *American Psychologist, 37,* 436–444.
Smith, M. L., & Glass, G. V. (1977). The meta-analysis of psychotherapy outcome studies. *American Psychologist, 32,* 752–760.

Chapter 5

The Case of Substance Abuse

Substance abuse is a serious problem in its own right as well as an excellent illustration of the complexity involved in defining abnormality, the changing conceptualizations apparent throughout history, the inherent difficulty of diagnosis and assessment, and the multiplicity of theoretical models, treatments, and research strategies. After reading this chapter, you should be able to do the following:

- Describe in detail alcohol abuse.
- Compare and contrast conceptualizations of alcohol abuse across the different historical eras of abnormality.
- Specify the strengths and weaknesses of each model of abnormality as applied to alcohol abuse.
- Know that highly effective treatments for alcohol abuse do not currently exist.
- Compare and contrast the other drugs subject to abuse (narcotics, stimulants, depressants, and psychedelics).
- Recognize examples of each of the classes of abused drugs.
- For each of the abused drugs, understand the characteristic symptoms of intoxication and withdrawal, prevalence, epidemiology (e.g., age, sex, and/or cultural differences), risk factors, explanations, and treatments.

Chapter Summary

Introduction

Psychoactive drugs affect brain activity and thus the nature of a person's consciousness. In seeking intoxication via psychoactive drugs, people may end up abusing these drugs.

Alcohol Use and Abuse

The most frequently abused drug today is certainly ethyl alcohol, the active ingredient in beer, wine, and liquor. Alcohol has a host of negative physiological and psychological effects on the individual, and alcohol abuse exacts an incredible toll on society's resources. Alcohol has been available for 10,000 years, and over this period, we see its use and abuse conceived in magical, somatic, and psychological terms. No consensus exists even today on whether alcohol abuse is a moral failing, a disease, or a bad habit.

Alcohol abuse proves difficult to define precisely, because people do not fall into discrete groups of users versus abusers. Relevant in judging abuse are such criteria as the amount of alcohol consumed, the pattern of use, physical consequences, social consequences, and loss of control over drinking. The diagnosis of drug problems involves several general issues concerning classification. What substances can be abused? Are there different types of substance abuse? If so, do they fall along particular dimensions? Does substance abuse share anything in common with other problems involving compelled behavior, such as gambling?

DSM-IV distinguishes between substance dependence, in which an individual experiences a variety of problems associated with drug use, and substance abuse, in which an individual experiences more circumscribed difficulties due to drug use. According to DSM-IV, 11 different drugs—including alcohol—may be associated with substance dependence and abuse. The assessment of substance use disorders can be difficult, because drug users are often unreliable sources of information.

The popular models of abnormality—the biomedical, psychoanalytic, cognitive-behavioral, humanistic-existential-phenomenological, family systems, and sociocultural approaches—have been applied to substance use and abuse. Each suggests its own view of the causes of substance use disorders and how best to treat them. Because there are reasonable and unreasonable aspects of each, an integrated perspective is needed.

The Use and Abuse of Other Drugs

Opium and its derivatives, such as morphine and heroin, are narcotics. These drugs produce an intense rush of pleasure followed by a lingering state of bliss. Illegal in the United States since 1914, narcotics are among the more commonly abused illicit drugs. Narcotics addiction is sometimes treated with substitution therapy, which provides the individual with an opiate such as methadone that is longer lasting and more gradual in its effects than heroin or morphine.

Stimulants are drugs that stimulate the nervous system, increasing arousal and spurring mental and physical activity. Caffeine, nicotine, amphetamine, and cocaine are included among the stimulants. The abuse of an extremely potent yet inexpensive form of cocaine known as crack increased greatly throughout the 1980s.

Depressants slow down the nervous system, creating a state of relaxation and temporarily ridding an individual of anxiety. The depressants include alcohol, tranquilizers, barbiturates, methaqualone, and inhalants such as glue, gasoline, and paint.

Psychedelics are drugs touted by their users as "consciousness-expanding," and include hallucinogens (e.g., mescaline, psilocybin, and LSD), phencyclidine (PCP), and marijuana.

GLOSSARY TERMS

addiction—physical dependence on a psychoactive drug, shown by tolerance and withdrawal

addictive personality—hypothesized set of traits that lead people to overindulge their appetites when anxious

alcoholic—according to the biomedical model of abnormality, individual with the disease of alcoholism; more generally, an alcohol abuser

Alcoholics Anonymous; AA—self-help group for recovering alcohol abusers

alcoholism—according to the biomedical model of abnormality, disease that leads people to abuse alcohol

amphetamine—synthetic stimulant such as Benzedrine

amphetamine psychosis—psychotic state characterizing acute amphetamine intoxication

antagonists—chemicals that block the effects of psychoactive drugs

barbiturates—synthetic depressants such as phenobarbital, prescribed to aid sleep

blood alcohol content; BAC—percentage of alcohol circulating in the blood

caffeine—stimulant found in coffee, tea, and chocolate

cocaine—stimulant derived from the leaves of the coca plant

codependency—relationship between a substance abuser and another person in which substance abuse is maintained because of the tacit aid and encouragement of the other person

controlled drinking—therapeutic approach to alcohol abuse in which the abuser is taught to drink in moderation

crack—potent and inexpensive form of cocaine produced by freebasing

cross-tolerance—tolerance to a psychoactive drug due to the repeated use of another psychoactive drug

delirium tremens; DTs—extreme form of withdrawal from alcohol, characterized by sweating, shaking, irritability, seizures, hallucinations, confusion, and disorientation

depressants—psychoactive drugs that reduce awareness of external stimuli and slow down bodily functions

detoxification—letting a psychoactive drug clear the user's body

Dionysus; Bacchus—Greek god of wine

disulfiram; Antabuse—drug that results in severe nausea and feelings of impending death when combined with even a single drink

endorphins—opiates produced by the brain that play an important role in the body's attempt to relieve pain

ethnic group—collection of individuals who share the same culture and regard themselves as belonging

to the same involuntary group
ethyl alcohol—active ingredient in all alcoholic beverages
hallucinogens—psychedelics that produce hallucinations
hashish—psychoactive drug derived from resin that exudes from the hemp plant
heroin—narcotic derived from morphine
inhalants—volatile substances such as glue, paint, and gasoline whose fumes can be inhaled to produce intoxication
intoxication—alteration in consciousness following ingestion of a psychoactive drug
LSD (lysergic acid diethylamide)—potent synthetic hallucinogen
marijuana—psychoactive drug derived from the leaves and flowers of the hemp plant
mescaline—hallucinogen derived from the peyote cactus
methadone—synthetic narcotic often used in substitution therapy
methaqualone—synthetic depressant similar in its effects to barbiturates
morphine—narcotic derived from opium
narcotics; opiates; opioids—opium and its derivatives, such as morphine and heroin
nicotine—stimulant found in tobacco
opium—psychoactive drug derived from the juice of the poppy
phencyclidine; PCP—synthetic hallucinogen originally used as a surgical anesthetic and analgesic
polysubstance dependence—use by a person of more than one drug at a time
psilocybin—hallucinogen derived from a particular species of mushroom
psychedelics—psychoactive drugs touted by their users as "consciousness-expanding"
psychoactive drugs—chemicals that affect brain activity and thereby the nature of consciousness
relapse prevention—attempt to prevent a return to drug abuse following treatment
stimulants—psychoactive drugs that stimulate the nervous system
substance abuse—symptoms indicating circumscribed impairment and distress due to drug use
substance dependence—symptoms indicating severe impairment and distress due to drug use
substance-induced cognitive disorders—demonstrable impairments of the brain and nervous system brought about by use of psychoactive drugs
substance-related disorders—behavioral problems associated with use of psychoactive substances
substitution therapy—treatment of narcotic abuse by substituting a longer lasting opiate that is more gradual in its effects than heroin or morphine
THC (delta-9-tetrahydrocannabinol)—active ingredient in marijuana
tolerance—need to take more and more of a psychoactive drug to produce the same effect
tranquilizers—synthetic depressants such as Valium and Librium, widely prescribed for anxiety disorders
withdrawal—alteration in consciousness following cessation or reduction of psychoactive drug use

NAMES AND DATES

Dionysus
Morpheus
Carry A. Nation (1846–1911)
Prohibition (1920–1933)

In general, know the historical trends in substance use and abuse.

Connections to Other Chapters

Chapter 5 attempts to illustrate ideas already discussed in previous chapters concerning the definition of abnormality (Chapter 1), historical perspectives (Chapter 1), diagnosis and assessment (Chapter 2), theories (Chapter 3), and research (Chapter 4).

Substance abuse frequently accompanies other psychological problems, as a risk factor (e.g., organic disorders—Chapter 6), symptom (e.g., antisocial personality disorders—Chapter 13), and/or consequence (e.g., fear and anxiety disorders—Chapter 7). One of the common findings in abnormal psychology is that different problems often co-occur. Substance abuse is one of the most frequently encountered problems associated with other difficulties. Indeed, it is difficult to identify an individual who has "just" a substance abuse problem, which means that the points raised in this chapter are often reintroduced when other psychological problems are the focus (Chapters 6-14).

Although strides have been made in the treatment of many disorders, substance abuse still proves highly resistant to most available treatments. It is worth pondering why these problems are so intractable. In any event, prevention of substance abuse may be the most reasonable goal for mental health professionals (Chapter 3).

Multiple-Choice Questions

1. The psychoactive drug about which psychologists know the most is:
    A. alcohol
    B. cocaine
    C. heroin
    D. marijuana
    E. Valium

2. Ethyl alcohol is the active ingredient in:
    A. beer
    B. liquor
    C. wine
    D. all of the above
    E. none of the above

3. Alcohol _____ the functioning of the nervous system.
    A. depresses
    B. does not affect
    C. excites
    D. makes irregular

4. Beer and wine date back at least _____ years.
    A. 2,000
    B. 4,000
    C. 6,000
    D. 8,000
    E. 10,000

5. _____ was the Greek god of wine.
   A. Achilles
   B. Dionysus
   C. Morpheus
   D. Venus
   E. Zeus

6. National Prohibition was decreed by the _____ Amendment.
   A. 12th
   B. 14th
   C. 16th
   D. 18th
   E. 20th

7. Alcoholics Anonymous is run by:
   A. clinical psychologists
   B. government officials
   C. psychiatrists
   D. recovering alcohol abusers
   E. social workers

8. The goal of controlled drinking is:
   A. abstinence
   B. coping with symptoms of withdrawal
   C. drinking in moderation
   D. ignoring the effects of intoxication
   E. not driving

9. According to the textbook, which of these is the single best definition of problem drinking?
   A. amount of alcohol consumed
   B. loss of control over alcohol use
   C. pattern of alcohol use
   D. physical consequences
   E. social consequences
   F. none of the above

10. According to DSM-IV, _____ is a more severe version of _____.
    A. substance abuse; substance dependence
    B. substance dependence; substance abuse
    C. substance dependence; substance use
    D. substance abuse; substance use

11. The current prevalence of alcohol dependence in the United States is about:
    A. 2%
    B. 10%
    C. 15%
    D. 20%
    E. 25%

50 Chapter 5

12. Alcohol abuse is heritable. This supports the _____ model.
    A. biomedical
    B. cognitive-behavioral
    C. family systems
    D. humanistic-existential-phenomenological
    E. psychoanalytic
    F. sociocultural

13. Antagonists are used by those who favor the _____ approach.
    A. biomedical
    B. cognitive-behavioral
    C. family systems
    D. humanistic-existential-phenomenological
    E. psychoanalytic
    F. sociocultural

14. According to psychoanalytic theorists, alcohol abusers have problems regarding:
    A. aggression
    B. death
    C. dependency
    D. obstinacy
    E. sexuality

15. Research _____ support the notion of an addictive personality.
    A. does
    B. does not

16. At least in the short run, alcohol intoxication is reinforcing. This supports the _____ model.
    A. biomedical
    B. cognitive-behavioral
    C. family systems
    D. humanistic-existential-phenomenological
    E. psychoanalytic
    F. sociocultural

17. Those who hold positive expectancies about alcohol use drink more than those who do not. This supports the _____ model.
    A. biomedical
    B. cognitive-behavioral
    C. family systems
    D. humanistic-existential-phenomenological
    E. psychoanalytic
    F. sociocultural

18. The mystical experience is a concept associated with the _____ model.
    A. biomedical
    B. cognitive-behavioral
    C. family systems
    D. humanistic-existential-phenomenological
    E. psychoanalytic
    F. sociocultural

19. Codependency is a concept that makes sense in terms of the _____ model.
    A. biomedical
    B. cognitive-behavioral
    C. family systems
    D. humanistic-existential-phenomenological
    E. psychoanalytic
    F. sociocultural

20. One's occupation is an important influence on the likelihood of alcohol abuse. This supports the _____ model.
    A. biomedical
    B. cognitive-behavioral
    C. family systems
    D. humanistic-existential-phenomenological
    E. psychoanalytic
    F. sociocultural

21. The textbook concludes that the _____ model provides the best explanation of alcohol abuse.
    A. biomedical
    B. cognitive-behavioral
    C. family systems
    D. humanistic-existential-phenomenological
    E. psychoanalytic
    F. sociocultural
    G. none of the above

22. The textbook concludes that the _____ model provides the best treatment of alcohol abuse.
    A. biomedical
    B. cognitive-behavioral
    C. family systems
    D. humanistic-existential-phenomenological
    E. psychoanalytic
    F. sociocultural
    G. none of the above

52 Chapter 5

23. Opium is an example of a:
    A. depressant
    B. narcotic
    C. psychedelic
    D. stimulant
    E. none of the above

24. Alcohol is an example of a:
    A. depressant
    B. narcotic
    C. psychedelic
    D. stimulant
    E. none of the above

25. Amphetamine is an example of a:
    A. depressant
    B. narcotic
    C. psychedelic
    D. stimulant
    E. none of the above

26. Caffeine is an example of a:
    A. depressant
    B. narcotic
    C. psychedelic
    D. stimulant
    E. none of the above

27. Cocaine is an example of a:
    A. depressant
    B. narcotic
    C. psychedelic
    D. stimulant
    E. none of the above

28. _____ is usually used in substitution therapy for heroin abuse.
    A. Antabuse
    B. Methadone
    C. Morphine
    D. Naloxone
    E. Opium

29. In recent years, smoking has increased among:
    A. females
    B. males
    C. teenagers
    D. both A and C
    E. both B and C

30. Ecstasy and ice are types of:
    A. amphetamines
    B. cocaine
    C. hallucinogens
    D. heroin
    E. tranquilizers

31. Inhalants are classified along with:
    A. amphetamines
    B. barbiturates
    C. cocaine
    D. opiates
    E. psychedelics

32. *Angel dust* is a synonym for:
    A. absinthe
    B. crack
    C. LSD
    D. marijuana
    E. PCP

Answers to Multiple-Choice Questions

1. A
2. D
3. A
4. E
5. B
6. D
7. D
8. C
9. F
10. B
11. A
12. A
13. A
14. C
15. B
16. B
17. B
18. D
19. C
20. F
21. G
22. G
23. B
24. A
25. D
26. D
27. D
28. B
29. D
30. A
31. B
32. E

Critical Thinking Questions and Research Paper Topics

1. The textbook describes five possible definitions of alcohol abuse. Can these be combined into an overall definition? Does the DSM-IV approach qualify as an overall definition?

2. Interpret the approach of AA to alcoholism in terms of the different models of abnormality. Why is AA effective for some people but not others?

3. Identify the reasons for Prohibition. Why did it fail?

4. Which approach to the treatment of substance abuse seems most likely to be successful? How can its effectiveness be increased?

5. Why has polysubstance abuse increased in recent years? Are some combinations more prevalent than others?

6. Trace the history of narcotics.

7. Trace the history of cocaine.

8. Why are men more likely than women to abuse drugs? Why are women closing the gap?

9. Compare the prevalence of alcohol use and abuse across cultures. What accounts for the marked differences?

10. At one time, psychedelics were proposed as a treatment for psychological disorders. What rationales were provided by proponents of psychedelic treatment?

11. Describe the abuse of prescription drugs.

12. The textbook sketches the basics of an integrative model explaining alcohol abuse. Do the same for one of the other drugs discussed in this chapter.

13. What would constitute an integrated treatment of substance abuse?

14. Why do many religions forbid the use of alcohol and other psychoactive drugs?

15. Should marijuana be legalized?

FURTHER READINGS

Bill W. (1976). *Alcoholics Anonymous: The story of how many thousands of men and women have recovered from alcoholism* (3rd ed.). New York: Alcoholics Anonymous World Services.

Brecher, E. M., & the Editors of *Consumer Reports*. (1972). *Licit and illicit drugs.* Mount Vernon, NY: Consumers Union.

Heath, D. B. (1990–1991). Uses and misuses of the concept of ethnicity in alcohol studies: An essay in deconstruction. *International Journal of the Addictions, 25,* 607–628.

Huxley, A. (1954). *The doors of perception.* New York: Harper & Row.

Johnson, H. (1989). *Vintage: The story of wine.* New York: Simon & Schuster.

Lettieri, D. J., Sayers, M., & Pearson, H. W. (Eds.). (1980). *Theories of drug abuse: Selected contemporary perspectives.* Rockville, MD: NIDA Research Monograph Series.

Marlatt, G. A. (1983). The controlled drinking controversy: A commentary. *American Psychologist, 38,* 1097–1110.

Marlatt, G. A., Baer, J. S., Donovan, D. M., & Kivlahan, D. R. (1988). Addictive behaviors: Etiology and treatment. *Annual Review of Psychology, 39,* 223–252.

Orford, J. (1985). *Excessive appetites: A psychological view of addictions.* Chichester, England: Wiley.

Peele, S. (1989). *Diseasing of America: Addiction treatment out of control.* Lexington, MA: Lexington Books.

Seligman, M. E. P. (1994). *What you can change and what you can't.* New York: Knopf.

Shedler, J., & Block, J. (1990). Adolescent drug use and psychological health: A longitudinal inquiry. *American Psychologist, 45,* 612–630.

Sher, K. J. (1991). *Children of alcoholics: A critical appraisal of theory and research.* Chicago: University of Chicago Press.

Vaillant, G. E. (1983). *The natural history of alcoholism.* Cambridge: Harvard University Press.

Weil, A. (1972). *The natural mind: A new way of looking at drugs and the higher consciousness.* Boston: Houghton Mifflin.

Zucker, R. A., & Gomberg, E. S. L. (1986). Etiology of alcoholism reconsidered: The case for a biopsychosocial process. *American Psychologist, 41,* 783–805.

CHAPTER 6

Organic Disorders

This chapter describes organic disorders: psychological problems associated with physical injury, illness, or defect. It is located early in the textbook to introduce basic ideas about the nervous system that will recur in subsequent chapters. After reading this chapter, you should be able to do the following:

- Describe the structure and function of the nervous system; that is, the brain and the network of nerve cells throughout the body.

- Specify the multiple ways in which the nervous system is integrated.

- Understand that organic disorders usually reflect a problem with one or more parts of the nervous system.

- Distinguish among the various organic syndromes, constellations of symptoms resulting from neurological damage or dysfunction.

- Define the various neurological problems with psychological consequences.

- Compare and contrast these problems in terms of symptoms, prevalence, epidemiology, causes, explanations, and treatments.

CHAPTER SUMMARY

Introduction

Organic disorders are psychological problems associated with physical injury, illness, or defect. Often the part of the body involved is the nervous system.

An Overview of the Nervous System

The nervous system includes the brain as well as the network of nerve cells throughout the body. It sets the parameters for behavior. The basic components of the nervous system are neurons, which communicate with one another by secreting chemicals called neurotransmitters. Neurons either excite other neurons to fire or inhibit them.

The brain contains the largest number and most dense concentration of neurons in the body. It consists of integrated layers; those near the top of the brain tend to regulate and direct those near the bottom. The nervous system is organized in multiple ways: spatially, biochemically, top to bottom, front to back, and laterally. The nervous system is also integrated with the endocrine system and the immune system.

Conceptualizing Organic Disorders

Unlike its predecessors, DSM-IV does not include organic disorders as a separate diagnostic category. However, it lists several cognitive impairment disorders that typically have organic causes.

Organic syndromes are common constellations of psychological symptoms resulting from neurological damage or dysfunction. They include: (a) delirium (global impairment of attention); (b) dementia (global impairment of cognitive functions); (c) amnestic syndrome (memory loss *not* associated with general cognitive problems); (d) organic personality syndrome (change in personality); and (e) intoxication and withdrawal (changes in brain function brought about by drug use or the cessation of drug use, respectively).

Neurological Problems with Psychological Consequences

Among the progressive neurological diseases are Huntington's chorea, Parkinson's disease, multiple sclerosis, and Alzheimer's disease. Multi-infarct dementia is a form of dementia caused by multiple strokes over time. Brain injuries caused by blows to the head can result in a variety of psychological difficulties. Brain tumors may similarly compromise normal functioning.

Tourette's syndrome is a neurological problem characterized by complex tics. One of the direct consequences of AIDS is a form of dementia called AIDS dementia complex. Korsakoff's syndrome is a form of memory loss that accompanies severe alcoholism. Untreated syphilis can result in a neurological condition known as general paresis that is marked by a host of cognitive difficulties. Epilepsy refers to a group of neurological disorders in which periodic bursts of neural discharge lead to seizures. Migraines are recurrent headaches characterized by nausea and a variety of other symptoms.

In many cases, actual cures of organic disorders do not currently exist, although various forms of rehabilitation can help the individual compensate for his or her losses.

Glossary Terms

acetylcholine—neurotransmitter linked to Alzheimer's disease

AIDS dementia complex—intellectual impairment caused directly by the AIDS virus

Alzheimer's disease—a progressive neurological disease characterized by forgetfulness, confusion, and loss of ability to care for oneself

amnestic syndrome; organic amnesia—memory impairment due to an organic cause

aphasia—problem stemming from brain damage and involving the inability to express and/or comprehend speech or writing

aura (preceding a migraine)—warning sign that a person is about to have a migraine headache

aura (preceding a seizure)—warning sign that a person is about to have a grand mal seizure

autonomic nervous system—the part of the nervous system that controls the heart, lungs, and digestive organs

biofeedback—operant conditioning therapy technique that helps a person learn to control abnormal bodily responses

central nervous system—the brain and spinal cord

cerebral cortex—the very outer layer of the brain

cerebral hemispheres—the two symmetric structures that comprise the cerebral cortex

cognitive disorder—DSM-IV term for a problem involving an alteration in consciousness or thought to which biological factors contribute

coma—complete loss of consciousness and responsiveness to environmental stimuli

confabulation—symptom of Korsakoff's syndrome: the filling in of memory gaps with imaginary events

coprolalia—symptom of Tourette's syndrome: the involuntary blurting out of obscene words

delirium—global impairment of thinking marked in particular by the inability to pay attention

delirium tremens; DTs—form of delirium caused by withdrawal from alcohol

dementia—global impairment of cognitive functioning marked in particular by problems with memory

dissociative amnesia—sudden memory impairment due to psychological trauma

dopamine—neurotransmitter linked to schizophrenia and Parkinson's disease

endocrine system—set of glands that secrete hormones

epilepsy—neurological disorder characterized by seizures

excitation—process by which one neuron causes another neuron to fire

focal seizure; partial seizure—seizure that disrupts the functioning of only part of the brain

forebrain—top layer of the brain

frontal lobes—brain structures located at the very front of the cortex and involved in the ability to plan ahead and anticipate the consequences of acts

functional disorder—problem resulting from abnormal experience imposed on normal brain structure and function

general paresis—psychological disorder and progressive analysis that results from untreated syphilis

generalized seizure—seizure that disrupts the functioning of the entire brain

grand mal epilepsy; generalized convulsive epilepsy—form of epilepsy marked by highly dramatic, generalized seizures lasting several minutes

hindbrain—bottom layer of the brain

hippocampus—structure of the forebrain thought to be involved in processing memories

Huntington's chorea—progressive neurological disease caused by a single dominant gene and characterized by bizarre movements and dementia

hypothalamus—brain structure that links the nervous system and the endocrine system

immune system—the body's defense against foreign material, such as germs

inhibition—the process by which one neuron causes another neuron not to fire

intoxication—changes in consciousness brought about by use of a psychoactive drug

Korsakoff's syndrome—a form of memory loss accompanying severe alcoholism, apparently caused by thiamine deficiency

midbrain—middle layer of the brain

migraine—recurrent headache marked by throbbing and pulsating pain and usually accompanied by other characteristic symptoms

multi-infarct (MI) dementia; vascular dementia—form of dementia caused by multiple strokes occurring over time

multiple sclerosis; MS—progressive neurological disease in which myelin deteriorates

myelin—white, fatty substance that covers and protects some neurons, allowing them to send their messages more rapidly

nervous system—the brain and network of nerve cells throughout the entire body

neuron—an individual nerve cell

neurotransmitter—chemical secreted by one neuron that affects other neurons

norepinephrine—neurotransmitter linked to depression

organic disorder—psychological problem caused by physical injury, illness, or defect

organic personality syndrome—lasting change in personality following neurological damage

organic syndrome—cluster of symptoms caused by neurological damage or dysfunction

parasympathetic nervous system—the part of the autonomic nervous system that counteracts arousal

Parkinson's disease—progressive neurological disease characterized by a tremor, rigid muscles, and an expressionless face

peripheral nervous system—the part of the nervous system that links the central nervous system to the muscles, glands, and sensory organs

petit mal epilepsy; generalized nonconvulsive epilepsy—form of epilepsy marked by generalized seizures lasting only several seconds

pituitary gland—the so-called master gland, which influences the secretions of many other glands

psychoneuroimmunology—field that studies the interrelations among psychological factors, the nervous system, and the immune system

rehabilitation—therapy that helps the individual compensate for loss of certain abilities by the development of new ones

seizure—uncontrolled and disorganized firing of a large number of neurons in the brain

serotonin—neurotransmitter linked to depression

somatic nervous system—the part of the nervous system that controls the skeletal muscles and sense organs

stroke—bursting or blocking of an artery that supplies blood to the forebrain

sympathetic nervous system—the part of the autonomic nervous system that produces arousal

temporal-lobe epilepsy; psychomotor epilepsy—form of epilepsy marked by focal seizures lasting several minutes

tic—an abrupt, rapid, and repetitive movement

Tourette's syndrome—neurological condition characterized by multiple tics
withdrawal—changes in consciousness brought about by cessation of a psychoactive drug

Names and Dates

Alois Alzheimer (1864–1915)
George Huntington (1851–1916)
Sergei Korsakoff (1854–1900)
James Parkinson (1755–1824)
Gilles de la Tourette (1857–1904)

Note that most of these individuals, all of whom described neurological diseases that now bear their name, were more or less contemporaries, reflecting the development of neurology as a discrete field in the 1800s.

Connections to Other Chapters

In covering organic disorders, Chapter 6 introduces important ideas about the structure and function of the nervous system. Subsequent chapters discuss neurotransmitter irregularities with respect to fear and anxiety disorders (Chapter 7), depression (Chapter 9), schizophrenia (Chapter 12), and autism (Chapter 14). Biological factors often figure in other disorders as well, including substance abuse (Chapter 5), mind-body disorders (Chapter 10), and some personality disorders (Chapter 13).

Despite the explicit biological underpinnings of organic disorders, these problems may still have indistinct boundaries (Chapter 1). Diagnosis and assessment are less than perfect endeavors (Chapter 2). And treatment of certain organic disorders is not possible in the sense of providing literal cures, so mental health professionals often focus on primary prevention (Chapter 3) and rehabilitation.

The population of the United States is aging, which means that many of the organic disorders described in Chapter 6 will increase in prevalence. Issues of an individual's competence to conduct his or her own affairs will thus become more salient (Chapter 15).

Multiple-Choice Questions

1. Organic disorders are an instance of _____ classification.
    A. categorical
    B. dimensional
    C. etiological
    D. symptom-based

2. The nervous system has in excess of 100 _____ neurons.
    A. thousand
    B. million
    C. billion
    D. trillion

3. The brain and spinal cord comprise the _____ nervous system.
    A. central
    B. parasympathetic
    C. peripheral
    D. somatic
    E. sympathetic

4. The somatic and autonomic nervous systems comprise the _____ nervous system.
   A. central
   B. parasympathetic
   C. peripheral
   D. sympathetic

5. The sympathetic nervous system is to the parasympathetic nervous system as:
   A. arousal is to relaxation
   B. brain is to spinal cord
   C. mind is to body
   D. thinking is to doing
   E. thinking is to feeling

6. When a neuron makes it more likely for other neurons to fire, this process is called:
   A. excitation
   B. inhibition
   C. metabolism
   D. regularization
   E. it depends on the neurons in question

7. When a neuron makes it less likely for other neurons to fire, this process is called:
   A. excitation
   B. inhibition
   C. metabolism
   D. regularization
   E. it depends on the neurons in question

8. The first layer of the brain to evolve was the:
   A. forebrain
   B. hindbrain
   C. midbrain

9. Characteristically human functions (e.g., language, abstract thought) tend to be located in the:
   A. forebrain
   B. hindbrain
   C. midbrain

10. The glands comprise the _____ system.
    A. central nervous
    B. endocrine
    C. immune
    D. peripheral nervous
    E. none of the above

11. The _____ is (are) considered part of the nervous system and the endocrine system.
    A. cerebellum
    B. cerebral hemispheres
    C. cortex
    D. hypothalamus
    E. pineal gland

12. The strong suit of neuropsychologists is:
    A. diagnosis
    B. prevention
    C. rehabilitation
    D. treatment

13. Organic disorders are often contrasted with _____ disorders.
    A. anxiety
    B. functional
    C. mood
    D. psychosomatic
    E. schizophrenic

14. A global impairment of thinking is called:
    A. amnesia
    B. delirium
    C. organic hallucinosis
    D. organic personality syndrome
    E. Parkinson's disease

15. The critical difference between delirium and dementia is whether:
    A. emotional expression is affected
    B. intellectual functions are compromised
    C. the cerebral hemispheres are impaired
    D. the condition is heritable
    E. the nervous system is intact

16. The actual genes responsible for _____ have been identified.
    A. epilepsy
    B. Huntington's chorea
    C. Korsakoff's syndrome
    D. Parkinson's disease
    E. Tourette's syndrome

17. Parkinson's disease is characterized by:
    A. contusions
    B. deficiencies in acetylcholine
    C. deficiencies in dopamine
    D. fluctuating GABA
    E. lacerations

18. Neural grafting has been proposed as a treatment for:
    A. epilepsy
    B. Huntington's chorea
    C. Korsakoff's syndrome
    D. Parkinson's disease
    E. Tourette's syndrome

19. Multiple sclerosis involves a problem with:
    A. acetylcholine
    B. dopamine
    C. GABA
    D. myelin
    E. the hippocampus

20. Alzheimer's disease is associated with the loss of neurons that communicate with:
    A. acetylcholine
    B. dopamine
    C. GABA
    D. norepinephrine
    E. serotonin

21. Multi-infarct dementia occurs _____ in life than Alzheimer's disease.
    A. earlier
    B. at the same time
    C. later

22. Damage to the frontal lobes interferes specifically with an individual's ability to:
    A. express emotions
    B. plan ahead
    C. remember distant events
    D. remember recent events
    E. all of the above

23. In modern societies, brain injuries are most common among:
    A. old females
    B. old males
    C. young females
    D. young males

24. Multiple tics are a symptom of:
    A. epilepsy
    B. Huntington's chorea
    C. Korsakoff's syndrome
    D. Parkinson's disease
    E. Tourette's syndrome

25. Problems with _____ seem to characterize Tourette's syndrome.
    A. acetylcholine
    B. dopamine
    C. both A and B
    D. neither A nor B

26. _____ is strongly associated with alcoholism.
    A. Epilepsy
    B. Huntington's chorea
    C. Korsakoff's syndrome
    D. Parkinson's disease
    E. Tourette's syndrome

27. _____ is characterized by seizures.
    A. Epilepsy
    B. Huntington's chorea
    C. Korsakoff's syndrome
    D. Parkinson's disease
    E. Tourette's syndrome

28. The most common treatment for epilepsy is:
    A. behavior therapy
    B. biofeedback
    C. drugs
    D. surgery
    E. none of the above

29. Auras may precede:
    A. migraines
    B. seizures
    C. both A and B
    D. neither A nor B

30. _____ is (are) more likely to occur in left-handers.
    A. Allergies
    B. Autism
    C. Mathematical ability
    D. Schizophrenia
    E. all of the above

Answers to Multiple-Choice Questions

1. C
2. C
3. A
4. C
5. A
6. A
7. B
8. B
9. A
10. B
11. D
12. A
13. B
14. B
15. E
16. B
17. C
18. D
19. D
20. A
21. A
22. B
23. D
24. E
25. C
26. C
27. A
28. C
29. C
30. E

Critical Thinking Questions and Research Paper Topics

1. Reductionism refers to the attempt to explain complex topics in simple terms. Do organic disorders exemplify reductionism? In other words, is it plausible to explain complex psychological problems *solely* in terms of damage to the nervous system?

2. What ethical issues are raised by the availability of genetic tests that predict whether someone is at risk for a given organic disorder?

3. Talk to a rehabilitation psychologist, and describe his or her typical day.

4. How can organic disorders be prevented in the first place? (Hint: See Chapter 3's discussion of primary prevention.)

5. How have imaging techniques refined the ability of neuropsychologists to diagnose organic disorders? What are the current limits of such techniques?

6. What is the relationship between Tourette's syndrome and obsessive-compulsive disorder?

7. Why is there a marked sex difference in the prevalence of most organic disorders?

8. Sketch how epilepsy might be explained in biopsychosocial terms.

9. Sketch how migraine headaches might be explained in biopsychosocial terms.

10. Describe recent attempts to reattach severed spinal cords. When, if ever, will this be a realistic treatment for spinal cord injuries?

11. Describe attempts to treat organic disorders with neural grafting.

12. Professional boxers sometimes suffer brain damage. What specific injuries occur? How might these be prevented or minimized?

13. Agree or disagree with the following statment: All instances of abnormality are organic disorders.

FURTHER READINGS

Coren, S. (1992). *The left-hander syndrome: The causes and consequences of left-handedness.* New York: Free Press.

Craufurd, D. I., & Harris, R. (1986). Ethics of predictive testing for Huntington's Chorea: The need for more information. *British Medical Journal, 293,* 249–251.

Jerison, H. J. (1973). *Evolution of the brain and intelligence.* New York: Academic Press.

Kolb, B., & Whishaw, I. Q. (1990). *Fundamentals of human neuropsychology* (3rd ed.). New York: Freeman.

Lezak, M. D. (1983). *Neuropsychological assessment* (2nd ed.). New York: Oxford.

Sacks, O. (1974). *Awakenings.* New York: Vintage.

Sacks, O. (1985). *Migraine: Understanding a common disorder.* Berkeley: University of California Press.

Sacks, O. (1985). *The man who mistook his wife for a hat.* New York: Simon & Schuster.

Springer, S. P., & Deutsch, G. (1985). *Left brain, right brain* (Rev. ed.). New York: Freeman.

CHAPTER 7

Fear and Anxiety Disorders

Fear and anxiety represent good examples of the continuity between normality and abnormality. They have their everyday counterparts familiar to us all, as well as extreme versions that can prove highly problematic. Chapter 7 describes disorders that are characterized by excessive fear and anxiety. After reading this chapter, you should be able to do the following:

- Describe the components of fear and anxiety.
- Define such fear and anxiety disorders as phobia, panic disorder, generalized anxiety disorder, obsessive-compulsive disorder, and post-traumatic stress disorder.
- Compare and contrast these disorders with respect to symptoms, prevalence, epidemiology, causes, explanations, and treatments.
- Describe how each of several theoretical models—biomedical, psychodynamic, and cognitive-behavioral—contributes to the explanation and treatment of these disorders.
- Critique each of these models.

CHAPTER SUMMARY

Defining Fear and Anxiety

Fear refers to the emotional, cognitive, physiological, and behavioral responses we make when specifically threatened. Anxiety refers to a similar complex of responses we make to nonspecific threats. There exist a number of disorders characterized by excessive fear and anxiety.

Phobia

A specific phobia is a persistent fear of a circumscribed object or situation. A social phobia is a persistent fear of being in a situation where some act must be performed under the critical scrutiny of others.

Panic Disorder

In panic disorder, the individual experiences recurrent attacks of panic: discrete periods of intense fear. Frequently occurring along with panic attacks is agoraphobia, the persistent fear of being in a situation from which escape is not possible.

Generalized Anxiety Disorder

Generalized anxiety disorder involves excessive and unrealistic anxiety cutting across a variety of life's domains.

Obsessive-Compulsive Disorder

In obsessive-compulsive disorders, people experience persistent obsessions—intrusive and disquieting ideas—or compulsions—repetitive acts carried out to prevent some dreaded consequence.

Post-Traumatic Stress Disorder

Post-traumatic stress disorder follows some traumatic event and is marked by a repeated reexperiencing of the trauma (via vivid recollections, nightmares, or flashbacks), reduced involvement in the external world, and diverse signs of anxiety.

Theoretical Perspectives

Several of the popular models of abnormality have a great deal to say about the origin and treatment of fear and anxiety disorders. The biomedical model attempts to specify the physiological mechanisms giving rise to fear and anxiety; a number of such mechanisms seem to exist. This model also tries to make sense of fear and anxiety disorders in terms of genetics and evolutionary theory, suggesting that these problems are extreme and perhaps outmoded versions of once adaptive reactions. Biomedical treatment relies on drugs. Tranquilizers are effective in reducing the symptoms of fear and anxiety. Imipramine, an antidepressant, is useful for combating panic attacks.

The psychodynamic model interprets the symptoms of fear and anxiety disorders in symbolic terms, as signs of underlying emotional conflicts that the person is unable to consciously acknowledge. This approach has the virtue of explaining why people tend to fear a narrow range of objects and situations; these have specific symbolic significance. Psychodynamic treatment aims at bringing unconscious material to light, presumably freeing the energy tied up in symptoms and making it available for other purposes.

The cognitive-behavioral model provides several perspectives on fear and anxiety disorders. One perspective views them as the product of simple conditioning. This approach is persuasive in many cases, and has inspired successful treatments, but nonetheless possesses certain explanatory shortcomings. A perspective that addresses these shortcomings while preserving the emphasis on learning theory suggests that these disorders are the result of prepared learning, conditioning predisposed by evolution. Another perspective provided by the cognitive-behavioral model explains fear and anxiety disorders as due to exaggerated beliefs about vulnerability; therapy from this viewpoint attempts to change these beliefs and replace them with more benign notions. The future will probably see an integration of these models to explain and treat fear and anxiety disorders.

GLOSSARY TERMS

agoraphobia—fear of being in a situation from which escape is not possible

anxiety—complex of reactions to danger that is unclear and/or diffuse

anxiety disorder—problem characterized by diffuse expectations of harm

benzodiazepine—tranquilizer such as Valium or Librium used to treat anxiety

buspirone—antianxiety drug that works by targeting serotonin

compulsion—repetitive act intentionally carried out in a stereotyped manner to prevent or neutralize some dreaded consequence

conditioning—the learning of simple associations

emergency reaction—response of the body to threat

endorphins—chemicals secreted in the brain that blunt pain

fear—complex of reactions—emotional, cognitive, physiological, and behavioral—shown in response to threat

fear disorder—problem characterized by expectations of specific harm

fixation—psychoanalytic term for an arresting of development

flooding—behavior therapy technique for treating fear and anxiety in which the individual is exposed repeatedly to the objects or situations of which he or she is afraid

free-floating anxiety—anxiety divorced from given events and circumstances

GABA (gamma-amino-butyric acid)—neurotransmitter involved in anxiety

generalized anxiety disorder; GAD—excessive and unrealistic anxiety that cuts across a variety of life domains

imipramine—antidepressant used to treat panic

modeling—behavior therapy technique for treating fear and anxiety in which the individual watches another person successfully confront the objects or situations of which he or she is afraid

neurotic disorder—problem marked by excessive anxiety, avoidance of problems rather than confrontation, and self-defeating tendencies

neuroticism; trait anxiety—tendency to be generally nervous or not

obsession—persistent idea, thought, impulse, or image that the individual experiences as intrusive, senseless, and disquieting

obsessive-compulsive disorder; OCD—disorder characterized by obsessions and/or compulsions

panic disorder—problem characterized by recurrent attacks of panic: discrete periods of intense fear

post-traumatic stress disorder; PTSD—disorder that follows the experience of a highly traumatic event, characterized by reexperiencing the event, avoiding reminders of the event, numbing of general responsiveness, and feeling anxious

prepared learning—learning predisposed by the evolutionary history of a species

repression—the active keeping of material in the unconscious

schema—a set of organized beliefs about some topic

social phobia—persistent fear of being in a situation where some act must be performed under the scrutiny of others

sodium lactate—chemical that builds up in the body during exercise, which can precipitate a panic attack among those vulnerable to them

specific phobia—persistent fear of a circumscribed object or situation

stress—reaction that takes place when a person tries to meet the demands of external events

systematic desensitization—behavior therapy technique for treating fear and anxiety in which the individual is taught to relax and then imagine objects or situations of which he or she is afraid, starting with mild images and moving gradually to more severe images

two process theory—Mowrer's theory of avoidance learning, in which an individual first learns through classical conditioning to fear certain stimuli and then learns through operant conditioning to avoid these stimuli

Names and Dates

Aaron Beck (1921–)

Sigmund Freud (1856–1939)

Pan

Martin Seligman (1942–)

John Watson (1878–1958)

Connections to Other Chapters

Psychological explanations of abnormality have long focused on disorders marked by fear and anxiety. Both Freud and Watson theorized extensively about such disorders (Chapter 1), and we thus should not be surprised that the psychoanalytic and behavioral models still have much to say about them. However, biomedical and cognitive approaches have also made important contributions to our understanding (Chapter 3).

Fear and anxiety characterize a number of disorders, including substance abuse (Chapter 5), certain organic disorders (Chapter 6), and somatoform and dissociative disorders (Chapter 8). The relationship between anxiety and depression is a particularly close one (Chapter 9). Some theorists have even called for a merging of the two diagnostic categories, arguing that the same sorts of events precipitate both. For example, threatened loss makes an individual anxious; actual loss makes the same person depressed. The difference here is chronological, not psychological. In any event, fear and anxiety are also apparent in many mind-body disorders (Chapter 10), sexual disorders (Chapter 11), schizophrenia (Chapter 12), and certain personality disorders (Chapter 13). Furthermore, fear and anxiety exist across the lifespan (Chapter 14) and are widely recognized across time and place.

Among the most effective treatments developed by mental health professionals include those for specific phobias (Chapter 3). The common ingredient seems to be exposure, either symbolically or actually, to what is feared.

MULTIPLE-CHOICE QUESTIONS

1. According to the textbook, fear and anxiety disorders _____ in degrees.
   A. exist
   B. do not exist

2. Fear shows itself in _____ domains.
   A. behavioral
   B. cognitive
   C. emotional
   D. physiological
   E. all of the above

3. The traditional difference between neurosis and psychosis involves:
   A. conscious mental processes
   B. estrangement from reality
   C. etiology
   D. prognosis
   E. the role of the central nervous system

4. Fear and anxiety disorders frequently co-occur with:
   A. academic success
   B. anger
   C. depression
   D. financial success
   E. schizophrenia

5. In specific phobia, people fear:
   A. concrete things
   B. particular behaviors
   C. wide-open spaces
   D. all of the above
   E. none of the above

6. In social phobia, people fear:
   A. concrete things
   B. particular behaviors
   C. wide-open spaces
   D. all of the above
   E. none of the above

7. In agoraphobia, people fear:
   A. concrete things
   B. particular behaviors
   C. wide-open spaces
   D. all of the above
   E. none of the above

8. Phobias are more common among:
   A. men
   B. women
   C. men and women equally

9. Panic attacks often accompany:
   A. agoraphobia
   B. social phobia
   C. specific phobia
   D. all of the above
   E. none of the above

10. Generalized anxiety disorder is more common among:
    A. men
    B. women
    C. men and women equally

11. Obsession is to compulsion as:
    A. emotion is to reason
    B. mind is to body
    C. reward is to punishment
    D. sympathetic nervous system is to parasympathetic nervous system
    E. thought is to deed

12. Less common today in obsessive-compulsive disorders than in decades past is a theme of:
    A. blasphemy
    B. contamination
    C. violence
    D. all of the above are less common today
    E. none of the above is less common today

13. Factors _____ trauma influence who develops post-traumatic stress disorder.
    A. before
    B. during
    C. after
    D. all of the above
    E. none of the above

14. Biomedical theorists stress the neurotransmitter _____ in their accounts of fear and anxiety disorders.
    A. acetylcholine
    B. dopamine
    C. GABA
    D. norepinephrine
    E. serotonin

15. Generalized anxiety disorder _____ heritable.
    A. is
    B. is not

72 Chapter 7

16. Two process theory is a concept associated with the _____ model of abnormality.
    A. biomedical
    B. cognitive-behavioral
    C. psychodynamic
    D. none of the above

17. Compulsion to repeat is a concept associated with the _____ model of abnormality.
    A. biomedical
    B. cognitive-behavioral
    C. psychoanalytic
    D. none of the above

18. Free-floating anxiety is a concept associated with the _____ model of abnormality.
    A. biomedical
    B. cognitive-behavioral
    C. psychoanalytic
    D. none of the above

19. Prepared learning helps explain the _____ of phobias.
    A. persistence
    B. rapid acquisition
    C. selectivity
    D. all of the above
    E. none of the above

20. Schema explanations of the fear and anxiety disorders stem from the _____ model of abnormality.
    A. biomedical
    B. cognitive-behavioral
    C. psychodynamic
    D. none of the above

21. Phobics usually have _____ experience with the objects they fear.
    A. had
    B. not had

22. In general, the most effective treatment of phobias stems from the _____ model of abnormality.
    A. biomedical
    B. cognitive-behavioral
    C. psychodynamic
    D. none of the above

23. Rape trauma syndrome is an example of:
    A. agoraphobia
    B. generalized anxiety disorder
    C. obsessive-compulsive disorder
    D. post-traumatic stress disorder
    E. specific phobia

24. Women with _____ sex roles may be at increased risk for fear and anxiety disorders.
    A. nontraditional
    B. traditional

Answers to Multiple-Choice Questions

1. A
2. E
3. B
4. C
5. A
6. B
7. C
8. B
9. A
10. B
11. E
12. A
13. D
14. C
15. A
16. B
17. C
18. C
19. D
20. B
21. B
22. B
23. D
24. B

Critical Thinking Questions and Research Paper Topics

1. Compare and contrast "normal" fear and anxiety with respect to their manifestations in fear and anxiety disorders. Do you agree that these represent a good example of continuity between normality and abnormality, or are the differences more than just those of degree?

2. Why are there sex differences in the prevalence of specific phobias? In other fear and anxiety disorders?

3. Why are there developmental differences in the sorts of things that are feared?

4. Why are there cross-cultural differences in the sorts of things that are feared?

5. Critically evaluate the preparedness explanation of phobias. For what does it *not* account?

6. Is obsessive-compulsive disorder chiefly biological? What about panic disorder?

7. Describe the psychological aftermath of torture or other instances of prolonged trauma. Judith Herman, in her 1992 book, *Trauma and recovery* (New York: Basic Books), suggests that post-traumatic stress disorder takes on different forms, depending on the extent of trauma. Evaluate her argument.

8. Is our contemporary society truly the Age of Anxiety? How could we demonstrate this conclusively?

9. Are there cross-cultural differences in neuroticism?

10. Why is exposure such an effective treatment for the various fear and anxiety disorders? Although usually identified as a behavioral approach, exposure can also be interpreted in terms of other models of abnormality. Which alternative explanations strike you as reasonable?

11. Is anxiety a cause or an effect of other disorders?

12. Describe the abuse of tranquilizers.

13. What is courage? Is it the opposite of fear? (See S. J. Rachman [1978]. *Fear and courage.* San Francisco: Freeman.)

FURTHER READINGS

Bandura, A. (1986). *Social foundations of thought and action.* Englewood Cliffs, NJ: Prentice-Hall.

Beck, A. T., & Emery, G. (1985). *Anxiety disorders and phobias: A cognitive perspective.* New York: Basic Books.

Eysenck, H. J. (1990). Genetic and environmental contributions to individual differences: The three major dimensions of personality. *Journal of Personality, 58,* 245–261.

Freud, S. (1909). Analysis of a phobia in a five-year-old boy. *Standard edition* (Vol. 10). London: Hogarth.

Freud, S. (1920). Beyond the pleasure principle. *Standard edition* (Vol. 18). London: Hogarth.

Gould, S. J. (1977). *Ontogeny and phylogeny.* Cambridge: Harvard University Press.

Herman, J. L. (1992). *Trauma and recovery.* New York: Basic Books.

Janoff-Bulman, R. (1992). *Shattered assumptions: Toward a new psychology of trauma.* New York: Free Press.

Marks, I. M. (1987). *Fears, phobias, and rituals.* New York: Oxford.

Prince, M. (1914). *The unconscious: The fundamentals of human personality normal and abnormal.* New York: Macmillan.

Rachman, S. J. (1978). *Fear and courage.* San Francisco: Freeman.

Rachman, S. J., & Hodgson, R. J. (1980). *Obsessions and compulsions.* Englewood Cliffs, NJ: Prentice-Hall.

Rapoport, J. L. (1989). *The boy who couldn't stop washing.* New York: Dutton.

Seligman, M. E. P. (1970). On the generality of the laws of learning. *Psychological Review, 77,* 406–418.

Seligman, M. E. P. (1971). Phobias and preparedness. *Behavior Therapy, 2,* 307–321.

Watson, J. B., & Rayner, R. (1920). Conditioned emotional reactions. *Journal of Experimental Psychology, 3,* 1–14.

Wolpe, J. (1958). *Psychotherapy by reciprocal inhibition.* Stanford, CA: Stanford University Press.

CHAPTER 8

Somatoform and Dissociative Disorders

Somatoform disorders are problems with physical symptoms that have psychological causes. Dissociative disorders are characterized by discontinuities, or breaks, in memory, consciousness, and/or identity. This chapter describes these disorders, which were at one time classified together. After reading this chapter, you should be able to do the following:

- Know why the psychodynamic model is often useful in explaining these disorders.
- Appreciate the difficulties of diagnosing somatoform and dissociative disorders.
- Describe such somatoform disorders as conversion disorder, hypochondriasis, somatization disorder, body dysmorphic disorder, and pain disorder.
- Compare and contrast these disorders with respect to symptoms, prevalence, epidemiology, causes, explanations, and treatments.
- Describe such dissociative disorders as dissociative amnesia, dissociative fugue, multiple personality disorder, and depersonalization disorder.
- Again, compare and contrast these disorders with respect to symptoms, prevalence, epidemiology, causes, explanations, and treatments.

CHAPTER SUMMARY

Introduction

In somatoform disorders, an individual shows physical symptoms such as pain, blindness, or deafness that seem to suggest the presence of an illness or injury, although none is present. In dissociative disorders, the person shows breaks in memory, consciousness, and/or identity that seem to suggest the presence of a neurological impairment, although again none is present.

These disorders are difficult to conceptualize because they are characterized by discontinuities. Often useful in explaining them is the psychodynamic model of abnormality, which views their symptoms as attempts to cope with threatening memories and impulses.

Somatoform Disorders

Several types of somatoform disorder exist. All must be distinguished from malingering, factitious disorder, psychosomatic disorders, and physical illness.

A conversion disorder involves the alteration or loss of physical functioning for psychological reasons: keeping a conflict out of awareness and/or achieving secondary gain. This disorder was long thought to be a physical disease afflicting only women. Freud was instrumental in arguing that it was psychological in nature and hence that it could affect men as well as women. Hypochondriasis is a preoccupation with having or contracting a disease, in the absence of any good reasons for this concern. Somatization disorder resembles hypochondriasis, except that the person complains about a greater variety of symptoms and fears a greater range of diseases. Body dysmorphic disorder is a preoccupation with an imagined defect in one's own appearance. Pain disorder is characterized by chronic pain in the absence of an adequate physical basis for it.

The somatoform disorders probably have a number of contributing causes, including enhanced physiological sensitivity to sensations, dire interpretations of these sensations, difficulty expressing emotions in words, social influences such as family style, actual traumatic events, and reinforcement of symptoms.

Treatments for the somatoform disorders take different forms, from reassurance and support to confrontation and setting limits. The more entrenched a disorder, the less responsive to treatment it is. Hypochondriasis and somatization disorder in particular resist treatment and have a chronic course.

Dissociative Disorders

Several dissociative disorders exist, and all can be understood in terms of the phenomenon of dissociation: the splitting of consciousness into two or more discrete streams, with little or no communication between them.

In dissociative amnesia, the person is suddenly unable to recall personally important information. This disorder occurs in the immediate aftermath of severe stress. Related to dissociative amnesia is dissociative fugue, in which a person loses his personal memory, travels away from home, and establishes a new identity under which he lives. Again, dissociative fugue occurs in response to stress. Multiple personality disorder (also called dissociative identity disorder) is a rare and fascinating problem in which different personalities exist within the same body, often unaware of one another. It is apparently much more common among women than men, and severe physical and sexual abuse during childhood is present in the vast majority of cases. Depersonalization disorder is characterized by episodes in which a person feels like an outside observer of his own thoughts and behaviors.

Like somatoform disorders, dissociative disorders are brought about by the interaction of several factors, notably trauma and the capacity for self-hypnosis. Although dissociation seems bizarre, the psychological mechanisms responsible for it may be quite mundane. When one segregates constellations of thoughts and feelings from one another, these may develop their own consciousness.

The dissociative disorders can all be treated by breaking down the barriers of amnesia that exist between dissociated states. Sometimes the mere passage of time accomplishes this, and other times the therapist must take steps to encourage the process. Prognosis tends to be good for the problems characterized by dissociation, including multiple personality disorder.

Glossary Terms

alexithymia—inability to express emotions in words

anxiety sensitivity—personality dimension reflecting the degree to which symptoms of anxiety are regarded as threatening

automatic processing—the carrying out of well-learned routines, cognitive or behavioral, without awareness

body dysmorphic disorder—preoccupation with an imagined defect in the appearance of a normal-appearing person

complex—constellation of feelings and impulses that influence behavior somewhat independently of the other aspects of a person

conversion disorder; hysteria—alteration or loss of physical functioning that suggests a bodily cause but instead is an expression of a psychological conflict or need

depersonalization disorder—recurrent and distressing feeling that one is an outside observer of one's own thoughts or actions

derealization—alteration of perception so that the external world no longer seems real

dissociation—a splitting of consciousness into two or more discrete streams, with little or no communication between or among them

dissociative amnesia—sudden inability to recall personally important information following psychological trauma

dissociative disorder—type of abnormality characterized by breaks in memory, consciousness, and/or identity without a physical cause

dissociative fugue—loss of personal memory, travel away from home, and establishment of a new identity following psychological trauma

factitious disorder—faking the signs of illness for no reason except medical attention

gate-control theory—an account of pain suggesting that its experience is regulated by as yet undiscovered "gates" in the spinal cord

histrionic personality disorder; hysterical personality disorder—personality disorder in which the individual is excessively dramatic, self-centered, and emotionally shallow and unstable

hypnosis—state of consciousness characterized by increased suggestibility

hypochondriasis—preoccupation with having or contracting a serious disease, in the absence of any medical reason for this concern

la belle indifférence—in conversion disorder, a lack of concern on the part of the individual regarding his or her physical symptoms

malingering—intentional faking of physical symptoms to achieve some specific goal

mass hysteria—individuals in a large group all showing the same groundless somatic complaint

Morita psychotherapy—Japanese treatment for anthropophobia

multiple personality disorder; MPD; dissociative identity disorder—existence within the same person of two or more distinct personalities—each with its own enduring and characteristic style—that alternate in taking full control of the person's behavior

nosophobia—simple phobia concerning illness

pain disorder—preoccupation with pain in the absence of an adequate physical basis for it

psychosomatic disorder—physical illness influenced by psychological causes

repression-sensitization—personality dimension reflecting a person's habitual response to disturbing occurrences; repressors tend to ignore these, whereas sensitizers tend to pay particular attention to them

secondary gain—achievement of reward or avoidance of punishment because of a symptom

somatization disorder; Briquet's syndrome—repeated concern with a variety of bodily complaints, in the absence of any medical reason

somatoform disorder—type of abnormality characterized by physical symptoms such as pain, blindness, or deafness without a physical cause

state dependent recall—tendency to remember information better when in the state during which it was originally learned

Names and Dates

Alfred Adler (1870–1937)

Pierre (a.k.a. Paul) Briquet (1796–1881)

Jean Charcot (1825–1893)

Sigmund Freud (1856–1939)

Pierre Janet (1859–1947)

Know the history of conceptualizations of somatoform and dissociative disorders, particularly conversion disorder (hysteria).

Connections to Other Chapters

Somatoform and dissociative disorders were at one time classified together as hysteria, which has long interested those concerned with abnormality (Chapter 1). Freud's first patients suffered from hysteria, and the psychoanalytic model still proves useful in explaining aspects of these disorders (Chapter 3).

The current view holds that anxiety lies under the surface of both somatoform and dissociative disorders. Accordingly, what has already been said about fear and anxiety in Chapter 7 applies here as well. Given the link between trauma and dissociative disorders, some believe that these disorders are closely aligned with post-traumatic stress disorder.

Somatoform-like symptoms often characterize other disorders, including substance abuse (Chapter 5), mood disorders (Chapter 9), sexual disorders (Chapter 11), and schizophrenia (Chapter 12). Dissociative symptoms may characterize organic disorders (Chapter 6), anxiety disorders (Chapter 7), and personality disorders (Chapter 13). This overlap of symptoms adds to the difficulty in accurately diagnosing somatoform and dissociative disorders (Chapter 2).

MULTIPLE-CHOICE QUESTIONS

1. Somatoform disorders consist of _____ symptoms with _____ causes.
   A. physical; physical
   B. physical; psychological
   C. psychological; physical
   D. psychological; psychological

2. Dissociative disorders are characterized by:
   A. discontinuities
   B. neurotransmitter abnormalities
   C. poor prognoses
   D. all of the above
   E. none of the above

3. Multiple personality disorder is classified as a _____ disorder
   A. dissociative
   B. somatoform
   C. both A and B
   D. neither A nor B

4. Conversion disorder is classified as a _____ disorder.
   A. dissociative
   B. somatoform
   C. both A and B
   D. neither A nor B

5. Body dysmorphic disorder is classified as a _____ disorder.
   A. dissociative
   B. somatoform
   C. both A and B
   D. neither A nor B

6. Depersonalization disorder is classified as a _____ disorder.
   A. dissociative
   B. somatoform
   C. both A and B
   D. neither A nor B

7. Briquet's syndrome is classified as a _____ disorder.
   A. dissociative
   B. somatoform
   C. both A and B
   D. neither A nor B

8. By definition, somatoform and dissociative disorders do not have _____ causes.
   A. any
   B. cognitive
   C. organic
   D. sociocultural
   E. unconscious

9. According to the textbook, the _____ model is often the most useful in explaining somatoform and dissociative disorders.
   A. biomedical
   B. cognitive-behavioral
   C. psychodynamic
   D. none of the above

10. When anxiety occurs in somatoform and dissociative disorders, it is often:
    A. manifest
    B. transient
    C. unconscious
    D. untreatable
    E. none of the above

11. Multiple personality disorder is _____ likely today than in centuries past.
    A. equally
    B. less
    C. more

12. Which of these does *not* involve faking?
    A. dissociative disorder
    B. factitious disorder
    C. malingering
    D. somatoform disorder
    E. both A and D
    F. both A and B
    G. both B and C

13. More common among women than men is:
    A. body dysmorphic disorder
    B. Briquet's syndrome
    C. dissociative amnesia
    D. both A and B
    E. both B and C
    F. all of the above

14. The onset of body dysmorphic disorder is usually during:
    A. infancy
    B. childhood
    C. adolescence
    D. early adulthood
    E. middle adulthood

15. Hysteria today is called _____ disorder.
    A. conversion
    B. body dysmorphic
    C. depersonalization
    D. derealization
    E. none of the above

16. According to Hippocrates, hysteria was caused by:
    A. a humoural imbalance
    B. a wandering womb
    C. faulty learning
    D. irrational beliefs
    E. neurotransmitter fluctuation
    F. unconscious sexual conflicts

17. *La belle indifférence* refers to the:
    A. chronicity of hypochondriasis
    B. comorbidity of somatoform and dissociative disorders
    C. inverse relationship between intelligence and height
    D. obliviousness of those with conversion disorder to their symptoms
    E. striking good looks of those with multiple personality disorder

18. Historically, hypochondriasis was considered a disorder of _____; nowadays it occurs chiefly among _____.
    A. men; men and women equally
    B. men; women
    C. women; men
    D. women; men and women equally

19. The symptoms of hypochondriasis are to those of somatization disorder as:
    A. accurate is to inaccurate
    B. bizarre is to mundane
    C. chronic is to transient
    D. few is to many
    E. sensory is to motor

20. Gate-control theory is an explanation of:
    A. consciousness
    B. dissociation
    C. hypochondriasis
    D. pain
    E. none of the above

21. _____ are prone to somatoform disorders.
    A. Repressors
    B. Sensitizers
    C. both A and B
    D. neither A nor B

22. Alexithymia refers to an inability to:
    A. express emotions
    B. learn abstractions
    C. move quickly
    D. sense colors
    E. think creatively

23. The prognosis is better for _____ disorders.
    A. dissociative
    B. somatoform
    C. both A and B equally

24. The notion of dissociation regards consciousness as:
    A. irrational
    B. nonexistent
    C. split
    D. submerged
    E. unconscious

25. Stressful events often precede:
    A. depersonalization disorder
    B. dissociative amnesia
    C. dissociative fugue
    D. multiple personality disorder
    E. all of the above

26. In _____, people know that memory has been lost.
    A. dissociative amnesia
    B. dissociative fugue
    C. both A and B
    D. neither A nor B

27. Multiple personality disorder is a problem experienced chiefly by:
    A. men
    B. women
    C. men and women equally

28. Childhood sexual abuse figures in _____ of cases of multiple personality disorder.
    A. 1%
    B. 5%
    C. 10%
    D. 50%
    E. 95%

Answers to Multiple-Choice Questions

1. B
2. A
3. A
4. B
5. B
6. A
7. B
8. C
9. C
10. C
11. C
12. E
13. F
14. C
15. A
16. B
17. D
18. A
19. D
20. D
21. B
22. A
23. A
24. C
25. E
26. A
27. B
28. E

Critical Thinking Questions and Research Paper Topics

1. What is the evidence for believing that anxiety is involved in somatoform and dissociative disorders?

2. Why is hysteria less common today than it once was? (Hint: See E. Shorter [1992]. *From paralysis to fatigue: A history of psychosomatic illness in the modern era.* New York: Free Press.)

3. Why are there cultural differences in the prevalence of somatoform disorders?

4. What might be done to prevent hypochondriasis or somatization disorder from developing in the first place?

5. Why is body dysmorphic disorder on an apparent increase in the contemporary United States?

6. Should dissociative fugue be considered a version of dissociative amnesia, or is it a discrete disorder?

7. Read one or more popular books about individuals with multiple personality disorder. How well do they fit the generalizations offered in this chapter?

8. Is multiple personality disorder a "real" phenomenon, or is there good reason to be skeptical? Consider both sides of the argument.

9. Why is pain so difficult to characterize and explain?

10. Some theorists argue that dissociative disorders are versions of post-traumatic stress disorder. Discuss the evidence for this theory.

11. Contrast conceptions of the self across culture and history.

12. Despite its rarity, multiple personality disorder receives a great deal of attention from professionals and everyday people alike. Why?

13. Should possession syndrome be considered an example of multiple personality disorder?

14. Should somatoform and dissociative disorders again be classified together?

FURTHER READINGS

Baur, S. (1988). *Hypochondria: Woeful imaginings.* Berkeley: University of California Press.

Bliss, E. L. (1980). Multiple personalities: Report of fourteen cases with implications for schizophrenia and hysteria. *Archives of General Psychiatry, 37,* 1388–1397.

Breuer, J., & Freud, S. (1895). Studies on hysteria. *Standard edition* (Vol. 2). London: Hogarth.

Ellenberger, H. F. (1970). *The discovery of the unconscious: The history and evolution of dynamic psychiatry.* New York: Basic Books.

Janet, P. (1920). *The major symptoms of hysteria.* New York: Macmillan.

Jaynes, J. (1976). *The origins of consciousness in the breakdown of the bicameral mind.* Boston: Houghton Mifflin.

Kellner, R. (1986). *Somatization and hypochondriasis.* New York: Praeger.

Kihlstrom, J. F. (1990). The psychological unconscious. In L. A. Pervin (Ed.), *Handbook of personality: Theory and research.* New York: Guilford.

Masson, J. M. (1984). *The assault on truth: Freud's suppression of the seduction theory.* New York: Farrar, Straus, & Giroux.

Podmore, F. (1963). *From Mesmer to Christian Science: A short history of mental healing.* New Hyde Park, NY: University Books.

Putnam, F. W. (1989). *Diagnosis and treatment of multiple personality disorder.* New York: Guilford.

Schreiber, F. R. (1974). *Sybil.* New York: Warner.

Shorter, E. (1992). *From paralysis to fatigue: A history of psychosomatic illness in the modern era.* New York: Free Press.

Thigpen, C. H., & Cleckley, H. (1957). *The three faces of Eve.* New York: McGraw-Hill.

Wolf, N. (1991). *The beauty myth.* New York: Morrow.

Chapter 9

Mood Disorders

The mood disorders are marked by pronounced alterations in mood. The two major mood disorders are unipolar disorder (or depression), characterized by depressive episodes, and bipolar disorder (formerly manic-depression), characterized by alternations of manic and depressive episodes. After reading this chapter, you should be able to do the following:

- Specify the symptoms of depressive and manic episodes.
- Explain the link between unipolar disorder and suicide.
- Describe the different types of depression.
- Understand how various theoretical perspectives contribute to the explanation and treatment of depression.
- Describe the different types of bipolar disorder.
- Know why bipolar disorder is viewed in biological terms.

Chapter Summary

Introduction

Mood disorders are problems characterized by alterations in mood. In depression, the person experiences excessive and inappropriate sadness. In mania, the person experiences excessive and inappropriate elation.

Depressive Disorder

Unipolar disorder (or depression) is characterized by depressive episodes, which affect all spheres of functioning: mood, thoughts, actions, and physiology. In our society, severe depression is closely linked to suicidal thoughts and attempts. More women than men attempt suicide, but more men than women succeed. The risk of suicide steadily rises as an individual ages.

Depression is one of the most common types of psychological abnormality. It runs through families, is more common among young adults than older adults, and is more common among women than men. Most episodes of depression lift on their own, after 3 to 6 months, but half of the time, another episode follows.

Biomedical approaches to unipolar disorder focus on the amine hypothesis: a theory proposing that depression results from insufficient activity of the neurotransmitters norepinephrine and serotonin. Stressful events and/or a genetic predisposition may be responsible for their low activity level. Biological treatments for depression attempt to increase norepinephrine and serotonin activity. Several strategies are successful, including drugs (tricyclics, MAO inhibitors, and Prozac), electroconvulsive shock therapy, and aerobic exercise.

Psychodynamic approaches to unipolar disorder emphasize the role of early loss in the life of the depression-prone individual, which creates excessive dependency and emotional neediness. Research support is equivocal at best. Interpersonal psychotherapy is a psychodynamic treatment that effectively eliminates depression. In this therapy, the focus is on interpersonal issues and conflicts.

Several cognitive-behavioral theories of depression exist. The behavioral theory of depression proposes that the disorder results from insufficient rewards in the environment, either because rewards do not exist or because the person lacks the skills to win them. Therapy from this view attempts to enrich the depressive's world and/or impart greater social skills. These strategies prove effective in alleviating depression. Learned helplessness refers to the maladaptive passivity that may follow exposure to uncontrollable aversive events. The individual who experiences uncontrollability in one situation comes to believe in his or her own helplessness, and this belief may then produce depression in other situations. According to the cognitive theory of depression, people become depressed as a result of excessively negative thinking that is maintained by erroneous logic. Cognitive therapy, which is another effective treatment for depression, proceeds by challenging these negative beliefs.

Biomedical, psychodynamic, and cognitive-behavioral models all contribute to our understanding of the causes and treatments of unipolar disorder. Each by itself is incomplete, and the future may well see an integrated approach.

Bipolar Disorder

Bipolar disorder (formerly manic-depression) is characterized by an alternation of depressive and manic episodes. In many ways, a manic episode has the opposite symptoms of a depressive episode; when manic, the individual is greatly elated, expansive, and energetic.

Theorists regard bipolar disorder as very much a biological problem. It is clearly heritable, and the treatment of choice is medication, specifically lithium, a naturally occurring salt that dampens mood swings. However, there is still a role for psychology in the conceptualization and treatment of bipolar disorder.

Glossary Terms

amine hypothesis—theory that depression results from an insufficiency of norepinephrine and serotonin

anergia—lack of energy

anhedonia—reduced interest and pleasure in the pursuit of everyday activities

automatic thoughts—unbidden and habitual ways of thinking

behavioral theory of depression—an explanation of depression proposing that it results from low levels of reward

bipolar disorder; manic-depression—mood disorder characterized by the alternation of episodes of depression and mania

Bipolar I disorder—bipolar disorder characterized by unambiguous manic episodes

Bipolar II disorder—bipolar disorder characterized by hypomanic but not manic episodes

cognitive theory of depression—explanation of depression proposing that it results from thinking negatively about the self, the world, and the future

cognitive therapy—Aaron Beck's therapy for depression in which the depressed client is encouraged to challenge his or her negative beliefs

cyclothymic disorder—a moderate version of bipolar disorder, in which the person alternates between mild depression and hypomania

dependent personality disorder—pervasive and excessive reliance on others for support and approval

depressive disorder; unipolar disorder; depression—mood disorder characterized by episodes of excessive and inappropriate sadness as well as a variety of other symptoms

depressive schema—constellation of negative beliefs and tendencies to process information in ways that maintain these beliefs, thought to cause depression

dysthymic disorder—mild yet chronic form of depression

electroconvulsive shock therapy; ECT—treatment for depression in which an electric current is briefly passed through the brain of an individual in order to induce a convulsion

endogenous depression—form of unipolar disorder characterized by somatic symptoms, psychomotor retardation, loss of interest in life, and lack of responsiveness to the environment

errors in logic—slipshod ways of thinking that keep negative beliefs immune to reality

explanatory style—a person's characteristic way of explaining the causes of events

flight of ideas—symptom of mania in which the person changes the topic of conversation from one to another to still another with great rapidity

hypomania—subdued version of a manic episode, in which the person shows an elevated mood and an increase in energy without any impairment in functioning

interpersonal psychotherapy—a therapy for depression that focuses on interpersonal issues and conflicts in order to help the individual get along better with other people

learned helplessness—maladaptive passivity that may follow exposure to uncontrollable aversive events
lithium—naturally occurring salt that controls both manic and depressive episodes of the bipolar individual
mania—enhanced mood and inappropriate sense of well-being
MAO inhibitors—class of antidepressant medication that presumably works by inhibiting monamine oxidase, the enzyme responsible for breaking down norepinephrine
medial forebrain bundle—the part of the brain involved in reward
melancholic depression—form of unipolar disorder dominated by bodily symptoms that are most severe in the morning
mood disorders—problems marked by alterations in mood
norepinephrine—a neurotransmitter thought to exist at an overly low level during depressive episodes
premenstrual syndrome; PMS—physical and psychological symptoms that occur during the late luteal phase of a woman's menstrual cycle
pressured speech—symptom of mania in which the person is unable to control his flow of words
Prozac; fluoxetine—antidepressant medication that presumably works by keeping the neurons that secrete serotonin from reabsorbing it
reactive depression; exogenous depression—form of unipolar disorder *not* characterized by the symptoms that mark endogenous depression
seasonal affective disorder; SAD—form of mood disorder in which moods show a regular relationship to the season, worsening in winter and lifting in summer
serotonin—a neurotransmitter thought to exist at an overly low level during depressive episodes
terminal insomnia; early morning awakening—inability to fall asleep after awakening
tricyclics—a class of antidepressant medication that presumably works by keeping the neurons that screte norepinephrine and serotonin from reabsorbing them

Names and Dates

Aaron Beck (1921–)

Emile Durkheim (1858–1917)

Charles Ferster (1922–)

Sigmund Freud (1856–1939)

Peter Lewinsohn (1930–)

Martin Seligman (1942–)

Know the history of how unipolar and bipolar disorders have been conceived.

Connections to Other Chapters

The mood disorders, particularly unipolar disorder, are among the most common of the psychological problems. Indeed, alterations in mood frequently co-occur with virtually all other disorders discussed in this textbook, including substance abuse (Chapter 5), organic disorders (Chapter 6), fear and anxiety disorders (Chapter 7), somatoform and dissociative disorders (Chapter 8), mind-body disorders (Chapter 10), sexual disorders (Chapter 11), schizophrenia (Chapter 12), and certain personality disorders (Chapter 13). Depression exists across the life span (Chapter 14), and it has been widely recognized across time and place (Chapter 1).

Changes in mood may variously be a cause, symptom, or consequence of all the other disorders just listed. In any event, a therapist can rarely afford to ignore the possibility of a mood disturbance or disorder. It is fortunate that effective means of treating both unipolar and bipolar disorder exist (Chapter 3).

MULTIPLE-CHOICE QUESTIONS

1. Whether a mood disorder is primary or secondary to another disorder depends on its:
    A. priority
    B. prognosis
    C. severity
    D. all of the above
    E. none of the above

2. Most basically, DSM-IV classification of mood disorders includes:
    A. depression and mania
    B. mild and severe disorder
    C. neurotic and psychotic depression
    D. temporary and chronic depression
    E. unipolar and bipolar disorder

3. The rarest of the mood disorders is:
    A. bipolar disorder
    B. depression
    C. mania
    D. all are equally common

4. The most common of the mood disorders is:
    A. bipolar disorder
    B. depression
    C. mania
    D. all are equally common

5. Unipolar disorder is characterized by _____ symptoms.
    A. behavioral
    B. cognitive
    C. emotional
    D. physiological
    E. all of the above

6. _____ attempt suicide more; _____ succeed more.
    A. Men; men
    B. Men; women
    C. Women; men
    D. Women; women

7. The opposite of reactive depression is:
    A. anaclitic depression
    B. bipolar disorder
    C. cyclothymic disorder
    D. endogenous depression
    E. hypomania

8. Most likely to be depressed in the contemporary United States are:
   A. adolescents
   B. children
   C. elderly females
   D. elderly males
   E. young adult females
   F. young adult males

9. About _____ of people recover from a depressive episode.
   A. 20%
   B. 40%
   C. 50%
   D. 75%
   E. 90%

10. Hippocrates explained depression in terms of:
    A. a wandering womb
    B. deficient neurotransmitters
    C. humoural imbalance
    D. illogical thinking
    E. uncontrollable events

11. The medial forebrain bundle is involved in:
    A. abstract thinking
    B. attention
    C. learning
    D. reward
    E. sleeping

12. _____ disorder is heritable.
    A. Bipolar
    B. Unipolar
    C. both A and B
    D. neither A nor B

13. The most controversial antidepressant is:
    A. chlorpromazine
    B. fluoxetine
    C. MAO inhibitors
    D. phenobarbital
    E. tricyclics

14. In terms of mortality, electroconvulsive shock is _____ than(as) antidepressants.
    A. less safe
    B. equally safe
    C. safer

15. Which treatment for unipolar disorder is most effective?
    A. antidepressants
    B. cognitive therapy
    C. electroconvulsive shock therapy
    D. interpersonal psychotherapy
    E. all of the above are equally effective

16. According to Freud, depression results from:
    A. anger turned inward
    B. excess anxiety
    C. illogical thinking
    D. psychotic defense mechanisms
    E. none of the above

17. Interpersonal psychotherapy is considered a _____ treatment.
    A. biomedical
    B. cognitive-behavioral
    C. family therapy
    D. psychodynamic

18. According to behavioral theory, depression is due to:
    A. illogical thinking
    B. low levels of reinforcement
    C. uncontrollable events
    D. all of the above
    E. none of the above

19. According to learned helplessness theory, depression is due to:
    A. illogical thinking
    B. low levels of reinforcement
    C. uncontrollable events
    D. all of the above
    E. none of the above

20. According to Aaron Beck's theory, depression is due to:
    A. illogical thinking
    B. low levels of reinforcement
    C. uncontrollable events
    D. all of the above
    E. none of the above

21. Explanatory style is a concept associated with:
    A. behavioral theory
    B. cognitive theory
    C. learned helplessness theory
    D. the amine hypothesis
    E. none of the above

22. Cognitive therapy of depression was developed by:
    A. Beck
    B. Ferster
    C. Freud
    D. Lewinsohn
    E. Seligman

23. Bipolar disorder has a lifetime prevalence of about:
    A. 1%
    B. 3%
    C. 5%
    D. 10%
    E. 25%

24. Hypomania is a _____ version of mania.
    A. maladaptive
    B. mild
    C. psychologically caused
    D. severe
    E. untreatable

25. The treatment of choice for bipolar disorder is:
    A. antidepressants
    B. electroconvulsive shock therapy
    C. interpersonal psychotherapy
    D. lithium
    E. tranquilizers

26. The textbook discusses a link between hypomania and:
    A. athletic achievement
    B. height
    C. increased longevity
    D. intelligence
    E. literary creativity

Answers to Multiple-Choice Questions

1. A
2. E
3. C
4. B
5. E
6. C
7. D
8. E
9. E
10. C
11. D
12. C
13. B
14. C
15. E
16. A
17. D
18. B
19. C
20. A
21. C
22. A
23. A
24. B
25. D
26. E

Critical Thinking Questions and Research Paper Topics

1. Does unipolar disorder have any basis in evolution? (Hint: Consider the possible benefits of mild depression in everyday life.)

2. Why are there historical differences in the symptoms that characterize depression? (See S. W. Jackson [1986]. *Melancholia and depression from Hippocratic times to modern times.* New Haven, CT: Yale University Press.)

3. Why are there cultural differences in the symptoms that characterize depression?

4. Why are there sex differences in the prevalence of depression? Be sure to consider explanations in terms of something about women and their lives as well as explanations in terms of something about men and their lives.

5. Why are suicide rates increasing among adolescents?

6. Why is suicide often considered immoral? Why is it often considered illegal?

7. Why are there cultural differences in the rate of suicide?

8. Why are children less likely than adults to be depressed?

9. DSM-IV describes a syndrome termed "premenstrual depressive disorder." Evaluate the pros and cons of including this category in a diagnostic system.

10. The textbook sketches an integrated explanation of depression. Taking off from this, describe what an integrated treatment might consist of.

11. Critically evaluate animal models of depression, such as the learned helplessness approach.

12. What is the evidence supporting the claim of cognitive theorists that cognitive characteristics precede depressive episodes?

13. Is Prozac dangerous?

14. Why do the various treatments of unipolar disorder appear to be equally effective?

15. The textbook links bipolar disorder with literary creativity. Describe similar evidence with respect to political leadership or musical achievement.

16. Discuss the difficulties in recognizing manic episodes among children.

FURTHER READINGS

Beck, A. T. (1991). Cognitive therapy: A 30-year retrospective. *American Psychologist, 46,* 368–375.

Beck, A. T., Rush, A. J., Shaw, B. F., & Emery, G. (1979). *Cognitive therapy of depression.* New York: Guilford.

Downey, G., & Coyne, J. C. (1990). Children of depressed parents: An integrative review. *Psychological Bulletin, 108,* 50–76.

Durkheim, E. (1897/1951). *Suicide.* New York: Free Press.

Ferster, C. B. (1973). A functional analysis of depression. *American Psychologist, 28,* 857–870.

Fieve, R. R. (1976). *Moodswing: The third revolution in psychiatry.* New York: Bantam.

Freud, S. (1917). Mourning and melancholia. *Standard edition* (Vol. 14). London: Hogarth.

Goodwin, F. K., & Jamison, K. R. (1990). *Manic-depressive illness.* New York: Oxford.

Jackson, S. W. (1986). *Melancholia and depression from Hippocratic times to modern times.* New Haven, CT: Yale University Press.

Klerman, G. L., Weissman, M. M., Rounsaville, B. J., & Chevron, E. S. (1984). *Interpersonal psychotherapy of depression.* New York: Basic Books.

Lewinsohn, P. M. (1974). A behavioral approach to depression. In R. J. Friedman & M. M. Katz (Eds.). *The psychology of depression: Contemporary theory and research.* Washington, DC: Winston-Wiley.

McKnew, D. H., Cytryn, L., & Yahraes, H. C. (1983). *Why isn't Johnny crying? Coping with depression in children.* New York: Norton.

Nolen-Hoeksema, S. (1990). *Sex differences in depression.* Stanford, CA: Stanford University Press.

Peterson, C., Maier, S. F., & Seligman, M. E. P. (1993). *Learned helplessness: A theory for the age of personal control.* New York: Oxford.

Schildkraut, J. J. (1965). The catecholamine hypothesis of affective disorders: A review of supporting evidence. *American Journal of Psychiatry, 122,* 509–522.

Seligman, M. E. P. (1975). *Helplessness: On depression, development, and death.* San Francisco: Freeman.

Taylor, S. E. (1989). *Positive illusions.* New York: Basic Books.

CHAPTER 10

Mind-Body Disorders

When psychological factors affect the onset or course of physical illnesses, we speak of mind-body disorders. Chapter 10 discusses these disorders in the context of the history of conceptualizations of how mind and body might be related. After reading this chapter, you should be able to do the following:

- Recount mind-body conceptualizations throughout history.
- Describe the roles played by social support and health promotion in physical illness.
- Know the components of the immune system and the goals of psychoneuroimmunology.
- Compare and contrast such mind-body disorders as cardiovascular diseases, cancer, gastrointestinal disorders, and asthma with respect to symptoms, prevalence, epidemiology, causes, explanations, and treatments, focusing on the involvement of psychological factors.

CHAPTER SUMMARY

Introduction

Psychosomatic disorders are physical illnesses influenced by psychological factors. Recent years have seen an explosion of knowledge about the psychological risk factors for illness as well as the mechanisms that lead from psychological states to physical well-being.

Minds and Bodies throughout History

A view across history shows that the relationship between mind and body has been conceived in drastically different ways. Early Greek thinkers like Hippocrates posited great continuity between the psychological and the physical, expecting each to influence the other. In contrast, French philosopher Descartes proposed that minds and bodies represented altogether different realms; minds were free, whereas bodies were determined. This mind-body dualism persisted into the 20th century, although eventually scientists came to regard both mind and body as subject to causes.

Medical practice reflected mind-body dualism. In the 19th century, physicians treated illnesses in heroic fashion designed to restore balance among bodily humours. Psychological factors were simply not part of the picture. Alternatives to orthodox medicine acknowledged the importance of psychological influences on illness, although these were short-lived with the growth of modern medicine, spurred by the proposal of germ theory. Once again, psychological influences on physical well-being were discounted.

Minds and Bodies More Recently

The 20th century saw psychological factors introduced back into the health and illness equation. Franz Alexander theorized within the psychoanalytic tradition about the possible link between emotional conflicts and illness. Hans Selye introduced an influential view of how all organisms, including people, responded to stress. Susceptibility to illness was one of the consequences of poor coping with stress. Subsequent researchers showed that psychological factors influenced the nature and extent of stress that people experienced. Cognitive factors are particularly important. Finally, the new field of psychoneuroimmunology took form, based on the explicit recognition that the nervous system, endocrine system, and immune system are in constant communication with one another.

Particular Mind-Body Disorders

The leading cause of death in the United States today is cardiovascular diseases, which have among their risk factors habits such as smoking and the Type A personality style: competitiveness, time urgency, and especially hostility. Fortunately, these risk factors can be altered with cognitive-behavioral interventions.

The second leading cause of death today is cancer, a family of diseases characterized by the uncontrollable growth of cells. Again, cancer has obvious behavioral risk factors such as smoking and drinking, as well as any behavior that brings a person into contact with cancer-triggering substances. Experimental studies with animals suggest that uncontrollable aversive events influence the growth of cancer cells. More controversial is whether personality factors influence the onset and/or progression of cancer. There is some evidence that people who are depressed and hopeless are at risk for cancer, whereas those with a "fighting spirit" are more likely to recover from it. Other studies have not found these links, so work on this continues.

Gastrointestinal disorders include gastroesophagal reflux (heartburn), peptic ulcer (a lesion in the stomach or duodenum), and irritable bowel syndrome (disturbances in defecation). Given behaviors may exacerbate all of these disorders. The role of stress and emotional conflict is less clear, although it does appear that peptic ulcers are made more likely by uncontrollable, unpredictable aversive events. Behavior therapy is helpful for treating the gastrointestinal disorders.

Asthma refers to a constriction of the airways to the lungs, resulting in hampered breathing. Among the psychological influences on asthma are conditioning, expectancies, and stress. Research has *not* supported earlier hypotheses explaining asthma in terms of a dependent personality style or an overly protective family. Behavior therapy, such as biofeedback, can be used to help alleviate the severity and frequency of asthma attacks.

Glossary Terms

antibodies—substances that destroy or deactivate antigens

antigen—any foreign material that invades the body and triggers the immune system

asthma—interference with normal breathing that occurs when the airways leading into the lungs constrict and fill with mucus

B cell lymphocytes—white blood cells, produced in bone marrow, that secrete antibodies

benign tumor—self-contained tumor, not composed of cancerous cells

cancer—a group of diseases characterized by uncontrollable growth of cells

cardiovascular diseases—diseases of the heart and circulatory system

chiropractic medicine—treatment of illness by manipulating bones and joints

dispositional optimism—the general expectation that good events will be plentiful in the future

explanatory style—how people habitually explain the causes of events

gastroesophagal reflux—passage of gastric juice upward from the stomach into the esophagus, where it creates a burning sensation

gastrointestinal disorders—problems of the gastrointestinal system

general adaptation syndrome—description of the stages involved in an organism's general reaction to any stressor: mobilization of resources, attempts to fight off the effects of the stressor, and—if resistance is unsuccessful—the depletion of resources and reduction of resilience to new stressors

germ theory—theory that all illnesses are caused by microorganisms known as germs

hardiness—ability to find meaning and challenge in the demands of life

Helicobacter pylori—bacterium that causes duodenal ulcers

heroic medicine—term for medical practice during the 1700s and 1800s, when extremely aggressive interventions such as bleeding and purging were routinely undertaken

homeopathy—treatment of illness by administering minute amounts of various drugs

immune system—bodily system that fights off infection by foreign material, notably germs

immunosuppression—sluggish or nonexistent response of the immune system to an antigen

irritable bowel syndrome; IBS—problem of the large intestine characterized by abdominal pain, disturbed defecation, and bloating or feelings of a distended abdomen

John Henryism—personality variable reflecting the degree to which a person believes that all events in life can be controlled solely through hard work and determination

malignant tumor—tumor composed of cancerous cells

metastasis—the spread of cancer cells throughout the body

mind-body dualism—philosophical doctrine that minds and bodies are separate realms with little or no influence on one another

natural killer (NK) cells—cells that directly kill cells infected with viruses as well as cancerous cells

peptic ulcer—lesion in the stomach or duodenum

phagocytes—cells that literally "eat" or engulf foreign material

popular health movement—18th-century social movement that urged people to take responsibility for their own health by learning more about their bodies and how to treat them

primary appraisal—the individual's assessment of what is at stake when a stressful event occurs

psychological factors affecting medical condition—DSM-IV term used to describe psychological factors coinciding in time with the beginning or worsening of a physical illness

psychoneuroimmunology—field that recognizes the mutual influences among psychological, neurological, and immunological factors

psychosomatic disorders—physical illnesses influenced by psychological factors

secondary appraisal—the individual's assessment of the resources at his or her disposal for meeting the demands of a stressful event

social support—the benefits that individuals provide for one another

T cell lymphocytes—white blood cells, produced in the thymus, that fight antigens in several ways, including killing foreign cells and stimulating the activity of phagocytes

tumor—a mass of cells

Type A coronary-prone behavior pattern—style of behaving linked to cardiovascular disease and characterized by strong competitiveness, time urgency, and hostility in the face of frustration

Names and Dates

Franz Alexander (1891–1964)

Aristotle (384–322 B.C.)

René Descartes (1596–1650)

Hans Eysenck (1916–)

Meyer Friedman (1910–)

Galen (130–200)

Hippocrates (460–377 B.C.)

Richard Lazarus (1922–)

Ray Rosenman (1920–)

Hans Selye (1907–1982)

Know the history of how mind-body relationships have been conceived. Be able to locate notable figures and events in time.

Connections to Other Chapters

Although the possibility that psychological factors contribute to physical illness has long been suspected, Western science for centuries entertained theories that all but precluded such influence (Chapter 1). More recently, with the advent of models that recognize the mutual influence of biological and psychological factors (Chapter 3), there has been a surge of interest in mind-body disorders.

Psychological risk factors and treatments have been described for these disorders. Anxiety (Chapter 7) and depression (Chapter 9) seem to be frequent precursors of physical illness, although we must be alert to the possibility that they also are common consequences. These psychological states influence illness not just directly through biological mechanisms (Chapter 6) but also indirectly through their influence on behavior.

Anxious or depressed individuals are less likely to do the sorts of things that prevent or limit physical illness.

The day may come when clinical psychologists are just as involved in the treatment of physical illnesses as they currently are in the treatment of psychological difficulties (Chapter 3). The fuzzy line between physical and psychological realms would have to be recognized (Chapter 1). More articulate theories that specify the mechanisms of mind-body disorders would have to be developed as well (Chapter 3). Perhaps "unhealthy" lifestyles will someday be described as personality disorders (Chapter 13).

MULTIPLE-CHOICE QUESTIONS

1. Mind-body disorders were once called:
   A. factitious disorders
   B. malingering
   C. neuroses
   D. psychosomatic disorders
   E. somatoform disorders

2. The textbook concludes that the _____ model of abnormality applies particularly well to mind-body disorders.
   A. cognitive-behavioral
   B. diathesis-stress
   C. family systems
   D. psychoanalytic
   E. sociocultural

3. Current opinion holds that the link between psychological states and illnesses is usually:
   A. general
   B. nonexistent
   C. specific
   D. theoretically possible but undiscovered
   E. none of the above

4. "A healthy mind in a healthy body" is associated with:
   A. Franz Alexander
   B. Aristotle
   C. Descartes
   D. heroic medicine
   E. Holmes and Rahe
   F. Hans Selye

5. Mind-body dualism is associated with:
   A. Franz Alexander
   B. Aristotle
   C. Descartes
   D. heroic medicine
   E. Holmes and Rahe
   F. Hans Selye

6. Bleeding as a treatment of illness is associated with:
   A. Franz Alexander
   B. Aristotle
   C. Descartes
   D. heroic medicine
   E. Holmes and Rahe
   F. Hans Selye

7. Alternatives to heroic medicine included:
   A. chiropractic medicine
   B. homeopathy
   C. the popular health movement
   D. all of the above
   E. none of the above

8. Germ theory took form in the:
   A. 1200s
   B. 1400s
   C. 1600s
   D. 1800s
   E. 1900s

9. The immune system was first described in the:
   A. 1200s
   B. 1400s
   C. 1600s
   D. 1800s
   E. 1900s

10. Foreign material that invades the body and is attacked by the immune system is called:
    A. antigens
    B. interferon
    C. lymphocytes
    D. NK cells
    E. phagocytes

11. The chief means by which the immune system fights off foreign material is via:
    A. B cell lymphocytes
    B. NK cells
    C. phagocytes
    D. T cell lymphocytes
    E. none of the above is primary

12. The founder(s) of modern psychosomatic medicine was(were):
    A. Franz Alexander
    B. Aristotle
    C. Descartes
    D. heroic medicine
    E. Holmes and Rahe
    F. Hans Selye

13. The general adaptation syndrome was proposed by:
    A. Franz Alexander
    B. Aristotle
    C. Descartes
    D. heroic medicine
    E. Holmes and Rahe
    F. Hans Selye

14. The pioneer(s) of life events research was(were):
    A. Franz Alexander
    B. Aristotle
    C. Descartes
    D. heroic medicine
    E. Holmes and Rahe
    F. Hans Selye

15. Research suggests that _____ is associated with good health.
    A. dispositional optimism
    B. nondepressive explanatory style
    C. both A and B
    D. neither A nor B

16. When someone dies, his or her spouse is at increased risk for death for a subsequent period of:
    A. 1 week
    B. 1 month
    C. 6 months to 1 year
    D. 5 years

17. The field that recognizes the mutual influence among psychological, neurological, and immunological factors is:
    A. ego psychology
    B. psychoneuroimmunology
    C. psychosomatic medicine
    D. the biopsychosocial model
    E. the diathesis-stress model

18. The leading cause of death in the contemporary United States is:
    A. asthma
    B. cancer
    C. cardiovascular disease
    D. gastrointestinal disease
    E. none of the above

19. The Type A behavior pattern is a risk factor for:
    A. asthma
    B. cancer
    C. cardiovascular disease
    D. gastrointestinal disease
    E. none of the above

20. Franz Alexander's theorizing about specific links between emotional conflicts and illnesses is supported by research with respect to:
    A. asthma
    B. cancer
    C. cardiovascular disease
    D. gastrointestinal disease
    E. none of the above

21. The critical ingredient in the Type A behavior pattern is:
    A. competitiveness
    B. hostility
    C. time urgency
    D. all of the above
    E. none of the above

22. The unchecked spread of cancer cells through the body is called:
    A. carcinoma
    B. leukemia
    C. malignancy
    D. metastasis
    E. reflux

23. Research _____ links stress to cancer.
    A. always
    B. sometimes
    C. never

24. Hans Eysenck cited studies from Yugoslavia linking _____ to the development of cancer.
    A. emotional repression
    B. helplessness
    C. hopelessness
    D. all of the above
    E. none of the above

25. Gastroesophagal reflux occurs when gastric juice enters the:
    A. esophagus
    B. large intestine
    C. small intestine
    D. stomach

26. *Helicobacter pylori* has been linked to the majority of _____ ulcers.
    A. colon
    B. duodenal
    C. gastric
    D. intestinal

27. In extrinsic asthma, the triggers for an asthma attack are:
    A. organic
    B. outside the body
    C. psychological
    D. removable

28. John Henryism is a personality variable used to explain increased rates of _____ among African Americans.
    A. asthma
    B. cancer
    C. cardiovascular disease
    D. gastrointestinal disease

ANSWERS TO MULTIPLE-CHOICE QUESTIONS

1. D
2. B
3. A
4. B
5. C
6. D
7. D
8. D
9. E
10. A
11. E
12. A
13. F
14. E
15. C
16. C
17. B
18. C
19. C
20. C
21. B
22. D
23. B
24. D
25. A
26. B
27. B
28. C

CRITICAL THINKING QUESTIONS AND RESEARCH PAPER TOPICS

1. Extrapolate the mind-body trends discussed in this chapter into the next century.

2. What role might clinical psychologists someday play in the prevention and treatment of physical disease?

3. Sketch the approach to treatment of Hippocrates.

4. Describe the development of homeopathy as an alternative to heroic medicine. Why does interest in homeopathy remain?

5. Describe the development of chiropractic treatment as an alternative to heroic medicine. What kinds of problems do chiropractors usually treat today?

6. Is the Type A style no longer a major risk factor for cardiovascular disease?

7. Describe an integrated treatment approach to cancer.

8. Describe an integrated treatment approach to asthma.

9. Migraine headaches (Chapter 6) are sometimes discussed as mind-body disorders. Evaluate this suggested classification.

10. Epilepsy (Chapter 6) is sometimes discussed as a mind-body disorder. Evaluate this suggested classification.

11. Eating disorders (Chapter 14) are sometimes discussed as mind-body disorders. Evaluate this suggested classification.

12. What can psychologists learn from public health about how to prevent mind-body disorders? Where does the analogy fail? (Hint: See Chapter 3.)

Further Readings

Ader, R. (Ed.). (1981). *Psychoneuroimmunology.* New York: Academic Press.

Alexander, F. (1950). *Psychosomatic medicine: Its principles and applications.* New York: Norton.

Barsky, A. J. (1988). *Worried sick: Our troubled quest for wellness.* Boston: Little, Brown.

Cohen, S. (1988). Psychosocial models of the role of social support in the etiology of physical disease. *Health Psychology, 7,* 269–297.

Cousins, N. (1976). Anatomy of an illness (as perceived by the patient). *New England Journal of Medicine, 295,* 1458–1463.

Eysenck, H. J. (1988). Personality and stress as causal factors in cancer and coronary heart disease. In M. P. Janisse (Ed.). *Individual differences, stress, and health psychology.* New York: Springer-Verlag.

Friedman, H. S., & Booth-Kewley, S. (1987). The "disease-prone personality": A meta-analytic view of the construct. *American Psychologist, 42,* 539–555.

Friedman, M., & Rosenman, R. H. (1974). *Type A behavior and your heart.* New York: Knopf.

Fuller, R. C. (1988). *Alternative medicine and American religious life.* New York: Oxford.

Lazarus, R. S., & Folkman, S. (1984). *Stress, appraisal, and coping.* New York: Springer.

O'Leary, A. (1990). Stress, emotion, and human immune function. *Psychological Bulletin, 108,* 363–382.

Peterson, C., & Bossio, L. M. (1991). *Health and optimism.* New York: Free Press.

Prokop, C. K., Bradley, L. A., Burish, T. G., Anderson, K. O., & Fox, J. E. (1991). *Health psychology: Clinical methods and research.* New York: Macmillan.

Selye, H. (1956). *The stress of life.* New York: McGraw-Hill.

Sontag, S. (1979). *Illness as metaphor.* New York: Vintage Books.

Stroebe, W., & Stroebe, M. S. (1987). *Bereavement and health: The psychological and physical consequences of partner loss.* Cambridge: Cambridge University Press.

Taylor, R. B., Denham, J. R., & Ureda, J. W. (1982). *Health promotion: Principles and clinical applications.* Norwalk, CT: Appleton-Century-Crofts.

Weil, A. (1988). *Health and healing* (Rev. ed.). Boston: Houghton Mifflin.

Chapter 11

Sexual Disorders

Sexuality is an obviously important aspect of human life. Perhaps not surprisingly, people may have difficulty with their sexual expression. Chapter 11 discusses the major types of sexual disorders. After reading this chapter, you should be able to do the following:

- Understand the importance placed by all societies on sexuality.
- Sketch the historical influences of early Christianity and Victorianism on contemporary Western attitudes toward sexuality.
- Sketch more recent events and figures in the history of sexuality.
- Describe the stages of the human sexual response and the role hormones play in human sexuality.
- Compare and contrast the common sexual dysfunctions in terms of their symptoms, prevalence, epidemiology, and causes.
- Sketch the different approaches to sex therapy.
- Explain the difficulty in defining, explaining, and treating paraphilias.
- Compare and contrast the different theories of sexual orientation.
- Describe what is known about the causes and treatments of transsexualism.

Chapter Summary

Introduction

Sexual disorders encompass sexual dysfunctions, which are problems with desire, excitement, activity, and/or orgasm; paraphilias, which refer to sexual activity with inappropriate individuals or in inappropriate circumstances; and gender identity disorder (or transsexualism), which involves inconsistency between an individual's gender identity and his or her anatomical sex. To understand problems with sexuality, we must understand sexuality itself and the great significance placed on sexuality by all societies.

A History of Sexuality

A view across history and around the world reveals great diversity in how sexuality is regarded. However, virtually all societies have strong codes about what is abnormal, illegal, and immoral.

The modern Western world has inherited its particular attitudes toward sexuality mainly from early Christian teachings that linked sexuality to sin and guilt. In the Victorian era, a strongly negative attitude toward sexuality resulted in widespread attempts to repress and deny its existence.

Starting with the theories of Freud, the 20th century saw sexuality regarded in an increasingly liberal and tolerant way. Part of this increased acceptance of sexuality was a willingness to study it scientifically. Kinsey undertook extensive surveys of "normal" sexual practices in the United States, and his results were important because of the variety they demonstrated within our society. Masters and Johnson studied sexual activity in the laboratory, providing the first good description of the physiological processes involved in the human sexual response. More recent influences on sexuality include the sexual revolution, feminism, the gay rights movement, and AIDS.

Sexual Function and Dysfunction

For both males and females, sexual response can be described as proceeding through four stages: excitement, plateau, orgasm, and resolution. Difficulties can occur at any of these stages, and DSM-IV describes sexual dysfunctions that involve problems with initial desire, continued activity, and/or the achievement of orgasm.

Sexual dysfunctions can have a variety of physical and psychological causes. Sex therapy as developed by Masters and Johnson is useful in treating sexual dysfunctions with psychological causes. This approach stresses information and communication, and it tries to get the couple to associate sexual activity with pleasure as opposed to anxiety.

Paraphilias

Sexual orientation refers to what an individual finds sexually arousing and what he or she wants to do during sexual activity. Paraphilias well illustrate the fuzzy boundaries of abnormality. Society deems some sexual orientations unusual and objectionable. Sometimes the objection is clear, as when a paraphilia involves inflicting pain on unwilling or nonconsenting individuals. In other cases, there is much more ambiguity.

The overall prevalence of paraphilias is unknown because of the secretive nature of such activities. These unusual sexual orientations are highly stable; they are found almost exclusively among males; they are sometimes associated with other psychological problems; their causes are largely unknown; and they are difficult to change with available therapy techniques.

Transsexualism

Transsexualism is a rare problem, although it attracts our attention because it challenges the way we think about gender and sex. The causes of transsexualism are not known, although when it exists, this problem is present throughout the individual's entire life. The only currently available treatment is surgery. A person's genitals are changed from female to male or vice versa in order to match his or her gender identity. This procedure is reportedly successful in two thirds of the cases, although critics have raised questions about this conclusion.

GLOSSARY TERMS

antiandrogens—drugs such as Depo-Provera that affect the pituitary gland so that the secretion of male sex hormones is inhibited

dyspareunia—recurrent pain in the genitals before, during, or after sexual activity

estrogen—a class of female sex hormones

female orgasmic disorder; inhibited female orgasm—persistent delay or absence of orgasm in a woman following normal sexual excitement and sexual activity judged "adequate" to produce orgasm

female sexual arousal disorder—persistent failure to attain or maintain the lubrication-swelling of sexual excitement until sexual activity is complete and/or a persistant lack of a sense of excitement or pleasure during sexual activity

gender identity—the experience of self as male or female

gender identity disorder—disorder characterized by a discrepancy between gender identity and anatomical sex

gender reassignment surgery—surgical treatment for transsexualism, in which male or female genitals are respectively refashioned into female or male genitals

hypoactive sexual desire disorder—persistent lack of desire for sexual activity

lovemap—hypothesized biological and psychological entity that functions as the "grammar" of sexual activity

male erectile disorder—persistent failure to attain or maintain an erection until sexual activity is complete and/or a persistent lack of a sense of excitement or pleasure during sexual activity

male orgasmic disorder; inhibited male orgasm—persistent delay or absence of orgasm in a man following normal sexual excitement and sexual activity judged "adequate" to produce orgasm

paraphilia—preferred or exclusive sexual activity with an inappropriate individual or in an inappropriate fashion

polymorphous perversity—Freud's term for the highly generalized sexuality of young children, who presumably can and do receive sexual arousal through the stimulation of many bodily parts

premature ejaculation—persistent ejaculation with minimal sexual stimulation and before the person wishes it

progestin—a class of female sex hormones

sensate focus—sex therapy technique that encourages the couple to stop paying attention to worries and stress—often about sexual performance—and instead focus on sensual pleasure

sexology—scientific study of sex

sex therapy—psychotherapy for sexual dysfunction

sexual aim—what an individual wishes to do with the sexual object

sexual aversion disorder—persistent aversion or avoidance of sexual contact with a partner

sexual dysfunctions—sexual inabilities: problems with sexual desire, excitement, activity, and/or orgasm

sexual object—the person or thing that an individual finds sexually arousing

sexual orientation—an individual's sexual object and sexual aim

testosterone—male sex hormone

transsexualism—gender identity disorder among adults

vaginismus—spasms of the vagina that make intercourse difficult or impossible

Victorianism—19th-century historical period characterized by widespread denial and repression of sexuality

NAMES AND DATES

Sigmund Freud (1856–1939)

Virginia Johnson (1917–)

Alfred Kinsey (1894–1956)

William Masters (1915–)

John Money (1921–)

Queen Victoria (1819–1901)

Locate in time the major events and figures in the history of sexuality.

CONNECTIONS TO OTHER CHAPTERS

As stated in this chapter, nowhere is there a better example of the fuzzy nature of abnormality than the category of sexual disorders. Ideas about normal and abnormal sexuality differ greatly across time and place (Chapter 1) and are frequently influenced by moral and legal pronouncements (Chapter 15). Sexual disorders seem to demand integrated models, given the number of influences on sexual behavior (Chapter 3).

Disturbances in sexual behavior frequently accompany other psychological disorders, including substance abuse (Chapter 5), organic disorders (Chapter 6), fear and anxiety disorders (Chapter 7), somatoform and dissociative disorders (Chapter 8), mood disorders (Chapter 9), mind-body disorders (Chapter 10), schizophrenia (Chapter 12), certain personality disorders (Chapter 13), and eating disorders (Chapter 14).

In recent years, there has been an increased recognition that sexual trauma can predispose psychopathology (Chapters 8 and 13). This forces our attention on the motives of those who perpetrate sexual crimes. What can be done to prevent or limit their actions (Chapters 3 and 15)?

Sexual dysfunctions can often be treated with success using the behaviorally based sex therapy of Masters and Johnson. In contrast, paraphilias often prove highly resistant to change, via behavioral or any other means. To date, sex-change operations—a biomedical approach (Chapter 3)—are the most frequent treatment of transsexualism, but they are controversial.

MULTIPLE-CHOICE QUESTIONS

1. According to the textbook, people in _____ cultures hold strong opinions and values concerning sexuality.
    A. all
    B. modern
    C. Western
    D. both B and C
    E. none of the above

2. Sexual disorders can be described as _____ problems.
    A. factitious
    B. mind-body
    C. neurotic
    D. psychotic
    E. somatoform

3. _____ is(are) more common among males than females.
    A. Paraphilias
    B. Sexual dysfunctions
    C. Transsexualism
    D. both A and C
    E. none of the above

4. DSM-IV locates sexual dysfunctions within:
    A. couples
    B. cultures
    C. individuals
    D. all of the above
    E. none of the above

5. Masters and Johnson locate sexual dysfunctions within:
    A. couples
    B. cultures
    C. individuals
    D. all of the above
    E. none of the above

6. The modern Western world has inherited many of its attitudes about sexuality from the early:
    A. Celts
    B. Christians
    C. Egyptians
    D. Greeks
    E. Romans
    F. versions of MTV

7. The Victorians _____ sexuality.
   A. celebrated
   B. denied
   C. mistrusted
   D. spoofed
   E. were indifferent to

8. _____ flourished in Victorian Europe.
   A. Child sexual abuse
   B. Pornography
   C. Prostitution
   D. Venereal disease
   E. all of the above

9. Freud theorized at the time of:
   A. feminism
   B. the AIDS epidemic
   C. the gay rights movement
   D. the sexual revolution
   E. Victorianism

10. The correct chronological order is:
    A. Freud ——> Kinsey ——> Masters and Johnson
    B. Freud ——> Masters and Johnson ——> Kinsey
    C. Kinsey ——> Freud ——> Masters and Johnson
    D. Kinsey ——> Masters and Johnson ——> Freud
    E. Masters and Johnson ——> Freud ——> Kinsey
    F. Masters and Johnson ——> Kinsey ——> Freud

11. Kinsey used _____ to study human sexuality.
    A. clinical case studies
    B. laboratory experiments
    C. surveys
    D. all of the above
    E. none of the above

12. Masters and Johnson used _____ to study human sexuality.
    A. clinical case studies
    B. laboratory experiments
    C. surveys
    D. all of the above
    E. none of the above

13. The so-called sexual revolution began during the:
    A. 1920s
    B. 1930s
    C. 1940s
    D. 1950s
    E. 1960s

112 Chapter 11

14. The gay rights movement is often said to have begun in:
    A. 1953
    B. 1957
    C. 1961
    D. 1969
    E. 1980
    F. 1992

15. Recent research suggests that _____ among males is(are) heritable.
    A. homosexuality
    B. paraphilias
    C. transsexualism
    D. all of the above
    E. none of the above

16. The first case of AIDS was diagnosed in the United States in:
    A. 1957
    B. 1966
    C. 1973
    D. 1981
    E. 1986

17. Testosterone is produced in the bodies of:
    A. females
    B. males
    C. both A and B
    D. neither A nor B

18. Hormones apparently have _____ effect on human sexual behavior.
    A. no
    B. some
    C. considerable

19. Hormones apparently have _____ effect on human sexual orientation.
    A. no
    B. some
    C. considerable

20. In order, the four stages of human sexual response are:
    A. excitement —> orgasm —> plateau —> resolution
    B. excitement —> plateau —> orgasm —> resolution
    C. orgasm —> excitement —> plateau —> resolution
    D. plateau —> excitement —> orgasm —> resolution
    E. plateau —> resolution —> excitement —> orgasm
    F. resolution —> excitement —> plateau —> orgasm

21. A refractory period after orgasm is more likely to be experienced by:
    A. females
    B. males
    C. both females and males equally

22. _____ are more likely to have a sexual pain disorder.
    A. Females
    B. Males
    C. Females and males equally

23. Sex therapy as developed by Masters and Johnson can be described as:
    A. behavioral
    B. cognitive
    C. psychodynamic
    D. psychoanalytic
    E. sociocultural

24. Masters and Johnson conclude that their sex therapy is effective _____ of the time.
    A. 10-20%
    B. 30-40%
    C. 50%
    D. 75%
    E. 80-90%

25. Which of these is *not* a paraphilia?
    A. exhibitionism
    B. pedophilia
    C. rape
    D. transvestism
    E. zoophilia

26. Sexual objects can be:
    A. people
    B. things
    C. both A and B
    D. neither A nor B

27. One hundred years ago in the Western world, paraphilias were described as:
    A. alternative lifestyles
    B. arrested development
    C. degeneracy
    D. illnesses
    E. normal
    F. sacred

28. Unusual sexual orientations _____ through families.
    A. run
    B. do not run

114 Chapter 11

29. Men with paraphilias _____ oversexed.
    A. are
    B. are not

30. In a state of polymorphous perversity, one is sexually stimulated via the:
    A. anus
    B. earlobes
    C. genitals
    D. mouth
    E. all of the above

31. Freud regarded homosexuality as a(n):
    A. alternative lifestyle
    B. arrested development
    C. degeneracy
    D. illness

32. Behaviorist explanations of sexual orientation emphasize:
    A. classical conditioning
    B. modeling
    C. operant conditioning
    D. schemas

33. John Money's notion of a lovemap is based on an analogy with:
    A. ethnicity
    B. grammar
    C. long division
    D. lower animals
    E. neurosis
    F. psychosis

34. A gender identity disorder in adulthood is called:
    A. a paraphilia
    B. homosexuality
    C. transsexualism
    D. transvestism

35. The causes of transsexualism are:
    A. biological
    B. environmental
    C. both A and B
    D. unknown

36. The treatment usually used for transsexualism is based on the _____ model of abnormality.
    A. biomedical
    B. cognitive-behavioral
    C. family systems
    D. psychoanalytic
    E. sociocultural

Answers to Multiple-Choice Questions

1. A
2. B
3. D
4. C
5. A
6. B
7. B
8. E
9. E
10. A
11. C
12. B
13. E
14. D
15. A
16. D
17. C
18. B
19. A
20. B
21. B
22. A
23. A
24. E
25. C
26. C
27. C
28. A
29. B
30. E
31. B
32. A
33. B
34. C
35. D
36. A

Critical Thinking Questions and Research Paper Topics

1. Suppose Christianity and Victorianism had not been as influential as they have been on our modern world. What might contemporary attitudes toward sexuality be in the Western world?

2. Does a repressive society encourage pornography?

3. Imagine AIDS never existed. How would the modern world be different, especially with respect to sexuality?

4. Agree or disagree with the following statement: Sex education should be taught in all elementary schools.

5. Compare the prevalence of sexual dysfunctions across time and place.

6. Critically evaluate the ethics of using sexual surrogates in sex therapy.

7. Are there any types of rape that should be classified as a paraphilia?

8. Why are paraphilias found chiefly among men?

9. The term *berdache* is used by anthropologists to describe aboriginal North Americans who filled an institutionalized role in which they were considered neither males nor females. How does this role challenge the way we think about gender? (See S. J. Kessler & W. McKenna [1978]. *Gender: An ethnomethodological approach.* New York: Wiley.)

10. Why have sex change operations been largely discontinued in the United States?

11. Critically evaluate Money's notion of a lovemap as an explanation of sexual orientation.

12. Homophobia is the irrational fear and dislike that some people have of homosexuals and homosexuality. Is this really a phobia? What are the origins of homophobia?

13. What issues are involved in the controversy about gays in the United States military? (Hint: Learn which countries have *no* ban on homosexuals serving in the military.)

14. Are paraphilias general or specific?

FURTHER READINGS

Bayer, R. (1987). *Homosexuality and American psychiatry: The politics of diagnosis.* Princeton: Princeton University Press.

Brownmiller, S. (1975). *Against our will: Men, women, and rape.* New York: Simon & Schuster.

Comfort, A. (1967). *The anxiety makers.* New York: Delta.

Ford, C. S., & Beach, F. A. (1951). *Patterns of sexual behavior.* New York: Harper & Row.

Gay, P. (1984). *The bourgeois experience: Victoria to Freud: Vol. 1. The education of the senses.* New York: Oxford.

Green, R. (1987). *The "sissy boy syndrome" and the development of homosexuality.* New Haven, CT: Yale University Press.

Kaplan, H. S. (1974). *The new sex therapy.* New York: Brunner/Mazel.

Katchadourian, H. A. (1989). *Fundamentals of human sexuality* (5th ed.). Fort Worth, TX: Holt, Rinehart, & Winston.

Marcus, S. (1966). *The other Victorians.* New York: Basic Books.

Masters, W. H., & Johnson, V. E. (1966). *Human sexual response.* Boston: Little, Brown.

Masters, W. H., & Johnson, V. E. (1970). *Human sexual inadequacy.* Boston: Little, Brown.

Money, J. (1985). *The destroying angel: Sex, fitness, and food in the legacy of degeneracy theory, Graham crackers, Kellogg's corn flakes, and American health industry.* Buffalo, NY: Prometheus.

Money, J. (1986). *Lovemaps: Clinical concepts of sexual/erotic health and pathology, paraphilia, and gender transposition in childhood, adolescence, and maturity.* New York: Irvington.

Money, J., & Ehrhardt, A. A. (1972). *Man and woman, boy and girl.* Baltimore: The Johns Hopkins University Press.

Shilts, R. (1987). *And the band played on: Politics, people, and the AIDS epidemic.* New York: St. Martin's Press.

Sontag, S. (1988). *AIDS and its metaphors.* New York: Farrar, Straus, & Giroux.

Stoller, R. J. (1985). *Observing the erotic imagination.* New Haven, CT: Yale University Press.

Storms, M. D. (1981). A theory of erotic orientation development. *Psychological Review, 88,* 340–353.

Wyatt, G. E., Peters, S. D., & Guthrie, D. (1988). Kinsey revisited, Part I: Comparisons of the sexual socialization and sexual behavior of white women over 33 years. *Archives of Sexual Behavior, 17,* 201–239.

Wyatt, G. E., Peters, S. D., & Guthrie, D. (1988). Kinsey revisited, Part II: Comparisons of the sexual socialization and sexual behavior of black women over 33 years. *Archives of Sexual Behavior, 17,* 289–332.

CHAPTER 12

Schizophrenic Disorders

Schizophrenia is one of the most severe psychological disorders. It is also one of the most controversial. After reading this chapter, you should be able to do the following:

- Explain the controversy that surrounds schizophrenia.
- Describe schizophrenia, its subtypes, and related syndromes.
- Understand the symptoms, prevalence, epidemiology, causes, explanations, and treatments of schizophrenia.
- Know why most contemporary theorists interpret schizophrenia in diathesis-stress terms.

CHAPTER SUMMARY

Introduction

Schizophrenia is a severe form of abnormality, characterized by patently false perceptions, a disorganized style of thinking, and neglect of the basics of living. This disorder has proved controversial, as theorists over the years have debated how to conceptualize it: as a discrete illness or as a biopsychosocial problem.

Symptoms, Subtypes, and Related Syndromes

To receive a DSM-IV diagnosis of schizophrenia, an individual must evidence psychotic epsiodes and deteriorated functioning for at least 6 months.

DSM-IV specifies several subtypes of schizophrenia: catatonic, disorganized, paranoid, undifferentiated, and residual. Perhaps more useful is the distinction between reactive and process schizophrenia, which reflects how rapidly or slowly symptoms develop, respectively, and is related to good versus bad prognosis, respectively. Another potentially useful distinction is between cases of schizophrenia in which positive symptoms such as hallucinations and delusions predominate versus those in which negative symptoms such as flat affect and social withdrawal predominate. These instances may have different etiologies and thus may require different treatments.

Several other disorders appear similar to schizophrenia. In schizophreniform disorder, schizophrenic-like symptoms are present but for less than 6 months. In schizoaffective disorder, the individual shows signs of both schizophrenia and mood disorder. Finally, a delusional disorder revolves around a firmly held false belief.

Epidemiology

The prevalence of schizophrenia is about 1 percent in most cultures around the world. It seems to occur equally among men and women, although recent studies challenge this conclusion. The disorder is more common among the lower class, and the relationship is particularly strong in large cities. It is primarily a problem of young adulthood and shows a variety of outcomes, from total recovery to chronic institutionalization.

Causes

Evidence suggests that schizophrenia has both biological and environmental causes. In biological terms, it is a heritable disorder associated with various neurological abnormalities. Theoretical attention has centered on the role of excessive activity of neurons sensitive to dopamine. In environmental terms, schizophrenic episodes may be foreshadowed and triggered by stressful events. Also, a family style of excessive emotional involvement and criticism bodes poorly for the long-term prognosis of the schizophrenic individual.

A full explanation of the causes of schizophrenia needs to encompass both biological and environmental factors, which appear to entwine in some way to bring about the disorder, perhaps by creating problems with how a person attends to stimuli.

Treatments

Chlorpromazine is a drug that controls the positive symptoms of schizophrenia. However, it does not affect the negative symptoms, and it may have a host of highly undesirable side effects. More promising as a treatment is clozapine, which effectively treats both positive and negative symptoms. Drug treatment of schizophrenia needs to be supplemented with psychological therapy, which can include psychodynamic treatment, behavior therapy, cognitive therapy, family therapy, group therapy, and milieu therapy.

Glossary

anhedonia—the state of being unable to experience any pleasure

catatonic behavior—grossly inappropriate bodily movement or posture

catatonic schizophrenia—a subtype of schizophrenia characterized by prominent catatonic behavior

chlorpromazine—drug frequently used to treat schizophrenia

clang association—characteristic of schizophrenic speech: stringing together rhyming words not otherwise associated

clozapine—drug used to treat both positive and negative symptoms of schizophrenia

delusion—a patently false belief

delusional disorder; paranoid disorder—a type of abnormality marked by a persistent, nonbizarre delusion, not due to any other type of psychological abnormality, such as schizophrenia

disorganized schizophrenia—subtype of schizophrenia characterized by incoherence, loose associations, and inappropriate affect, without systematized delusions or hallucinations

dopamine hypothesis—theory that schizophrenia is caused by excess activity of the neurotransmitter dopamine

expressed emotion; EE—degree to which family members are emotionally overinvolved and excessively critical of one another

extrapyramidal symptoms—common side effects of antipsychotic medication, akin to the movement disturbances that characterize Parkinson's disease

flat affect—lack of expressed emotion

hallucination—sensory experience that no one else confirms or supports

lobotomy—surgical procedure in which nerve fibers connecting the frontal lobes of the brain to the thalamus are severed; formerly used to treat schizophrenia

loose association—difficult-to-follow transition between two topics

milieu therapy—the organization of a total treatment system to facilitate improvement of individuals

negative symptoms (of schizophrenia)—flat affect, anhedonia, and social withdrawal

neologism—a coined word

paranoid schizophrenia—subtype of schizophrenia characterized by prominent and systematized delusions or frequent auditory hallucinations centering on the same theme

positive symptoms (of schizophrenia)—flagrant signs of psychosis, such as hallucinations, delusions, and disordered thinking

process schizophrenia—type of schizophrenia in which symptoms come over a person gradually, with no obvious precipitant

reactive schizophrenia—type of schizophrenia in which symptoms occur suddenly to a person, in response to some stressful event in the environment

residual schizophrenia—subtype of schizophrenia used to describe individuals who at one time met the diagnostic criteria for schizophrenia and at present no longer do, but continue to evidence mild signs of some schizophrenic symptoms

schizoaffective disorder—type of abnormality in which the individual satisfies the criteria for a depressive or manic episode as well as the criteria for a psychotic episode

schizophrenia—type of abnormality characterized by false sensations, perceptions, and beliefs, a disorganized style of thinking, and neglect of the basics of living

schizophrenia spectrum disorders—the range of disorders that appear related to schizophrenia

schizophreniform disorder—type of abnormality characterized by schizophrenic-like symptoms that last for less than 6 months

serotonin—neurotransmitter thought to be involved in schizophrenia and affected by clozapine

tardive dyskinesia—possible side effect of antipsychotic medication: involuntary movements of the lips, tongue, and face

token economy—behavior therapy carried out on an entire hospital ward, in which patients earn tokens for desirable behaviors and lose them for negative behaviors—with the tokens then exchanged for commodities

undifferentiated schizophrenia—subtype of schizophrenia used to describe individuals who cannot be diagnosed clearly as catatonic, disorganized, or paranoid

waxy flexibility—when the limbs of a catatonic individual can be moved slowly into a particular position, which is then maintained, sometimes for hours

word salad—metaphor describing schizophrenic speech, used to convey the idea that a schizophrenic's words may come out as a tumble

NAMES AND DATES

Gregory Bateson (1904–1980)

Eugen Bleuler (1857–1939)

Erving Goffman (1922–1982)

Ronald Laing (1927–1989)

Eges Moniz (1874–1955)

Thomas Szasz (1920–)

Know the history of how schizophrenia has been explained and treated over the years.

CONNECTIONS TO OTHER CHAPTERS

In its extreme, schizophrenia is an excellent example of what is meant by abnormality (Chapter 1). However, there is no lack of controversy about how to diagnose (Chapter 2) and explain (Chapter 3) this serious disorder. Many theorists today believe that schizophrenia is best viewed in diathesis-stress terms, which means that contemporary accounts of schizophrenia can serve as an example of how to explain other disorders (e.g., substance abuse—Chapter 5; mood disorders—Chapter 9; sexual disorders—Chapter 11) in these terms.

In recent years, the concept of schizophrenia spectrum disorders has been introduced. It is based on the assumption that schizophrenia shares important characteristics in common with certain organic disorders (Chapter 6), mood disorders (Chapter 9), and personality disorders (Chapter 13). As researchers undertake explicit comparisons and contrasts across the schizophrenia spectrum (Chapter 4), perhaps new insights into all of these disorders will emerge.

The introduction of the major tranquilizers in the 1950s as a treatment of schizophrenia represented a great step forward (Chapter 3). The population of mental hospitals was dramatically reduced over the next few decades (Chapter 15). However, it is apparent that drugs do not represent the whole treatment story. Psychological interventions must be used to supplement the major tranquilizers, and the plight of former mental patients in the wake of deinstitutionalization must also be addressed. Further, much more needs to be learned about the primary, secondary, and tertiary prevention of schizophrenia (Chapter 3).

When the legal system interacts with abnormality, it is often with respect to those suffering from schizophrenia (Chapter 15). Many patients in mental hospitals are diagnosed with the disorder, as are a number of those who offer an insanity plea when charged with crimes.

Multiple-Choice Questions

1. The textbook describes schizophrenia as:
   A. heterogeneous
   B. noncontroversial
   C. nonserious
   D. progressive
   E. well understood

2. Schizophrenia spectrum disorders include:
   A. schizoaffective disorder
   B. schizophrenia
   C. schizophreniform disorder
   D. all of the above
   E. none of the above

3. The central debate about schizophrenia concerns its:
   A. conceptualization as a discrete disease
   B. existence in females
   C. existence in males
   D. status as a disorder
   E. treatment with drugs

4. Which of these is *not* a myth about schizophrenia?
   A. Schizophrenics are constantly out of control.
   B. Schizophrenics are dangerous.
   C. Schizophrenics have a split personality.
   D. All of these are myths.
   E. None of these is a myth.

5. Schizophrenia _____ heritable.
   A. is
   B. is not
   C. it depends on the subtype

6. To meet DSM-IV criteria for schizophrenia, an individual must show:
   A. psychotic symptoms
   B. deteriorated self-care
   C. symptom duration of 6 months
   D. all of the above
   E. none of the above

7. The subtype of schizophrenia characterized by grossly inappropriate motor behavior is _____ schizophrenia.
   A. catatonic
   B. disorganized
   C. paranoid
   D. residual
   E. undifferentiated

8. The subtype of schizophrenia characterized by incoherence and inappropriate affect is _____ schizophrenia.
   A. catatonic
   B. disorganized
   C. paranoid
   D. residual
   E. undifferentiated

9. The subtype of schizophrenia characterized by systematized delusions is _____ schizophrenia.
   A. catatonic
   B. disorganized
   C. paranoid
   D. residual
   E. undifferentiated

10. The prognosis for _____ schizophrenia is better.
    A. process
    B. reactive
    C. process and reactive equally

11. Hallucinations and delusions are examples of _____ symptoms of schizophrenia.
    A. negative
    B. positive
    C. both A and B
    D. neither A nor B

12. If schizophrenic-like symptoms last for fewer than 6 months, the appropriate diagnosis is:
    A. delusional disorder
    B. schizoaffective disorder
    C. schizophrenia
    D. schizophreniform disorder
    E. schizotypal personality disorder

13. Schizoaffective disorder appears to be a combination of symptoms of schizophrenia with those of:
    A. bipolar disorder
    B. obsessive-compulsive disorder
    C. substance abuse
    D. transsexualism
    E. any or all of the above

14. The symptoms of delusional disorder are often interpreted in terms of:
    A. boredom
    B. defenses
    C. mental retardation
    D. modeling
    E. secondary gain

15. The lifetime prevalence of schizophrenia is about:
    A. 1%
    B. 3%
    C. 5%
    D. 7%
    E. 9%

16. Schizophrenia tends to occur for the first time at an earlier age for:
    A. males
    B. females
    C. males and females equally

17. About _____ of those diagnosed with schizophrenia eventually make a full recovery.
    A. 1–5%
    B. 10%
    C. 20%
    D. 50%
    E. 75–90%

18. Schizophrenia has _____ risk factors.
    A. biological
    B. environmental
    C. both A and B
    D. neither A nor B

19. The neurotransmitter usually implicated in schizophrenia is:
    A. acetylcholine
    B. dopamine
    C. GABA
    D. norepinephrine
    E. serotonin

20. Increased neurotransmitter activity characterizes _____ symptoms of schizophrenia.
    A. negative
    B. positive
    C. both A and B
    D. neither A nor B

21. Typical neuroleptics treat _____ symptoms of schizophrenia.
    A. negative
    B. positive
    C. both A and B
    D. neither A nor B

22. A condition that looks very much like an acute schizophrenic episode can be produced by chronic use of:
    A. alcohol
    B. amphetamines
    C. barbiturates
    D. marijuana
    E. narcotics

23. Research links high levels of expressed emotion within a family to the _____ of schizophrenia.
    A. onset
    B. prognosis
    C. both A and B
    D. neither A nor B

24. Schizophrenia appears to involve a problem with _____ attention.
    A. fluctuating
    B. illogical
    C. nonexistent
    D. overly inclusive
    E. none of the above

25. Lobotomies are _____ treatments of schizophrenia.
    A. effective
    B. ineffective

26. Clozapine seems to help _____ symptoms of schizophrenia.
    A. negative
    B. positive
    C. both A and B
    D. neither A nor B

27. According to the textbook, drug treatment of schizophrenia:
    A. is rarely undertaken
    B. is sufficient
    C. must be supplemented with psychological treatment
    D. should be discontinued

28. Unambiguous written descriptions of schizophrenia appeared for the first time in the _____ century.
    A. 11th
    B. 13th
    C. 15th
    D. 17th
    E. none of the above—descriptions have existed as long as there have been written records

Answers to Multiple-Choice Questions

1. A
2. D
3. A
4. D
5. A
6. D
7. A
8. B
9. C
10. B
11. B
12. D
13. A
14. B
15. A
16. A
17. C
18. C
19. B
20. B
21. B
22. B
23. B
24. D
25. B
26. C
27. C
28. D

Critical Thinking Questions and Research Paper Topics

1. Read about the Genain quadruplets (e.g., D. Rosenthal [Ed.]. [1963]. *The Genain quadruplets.* New York: Basic Books). How well do they fit the generalizations offered here about schizophrenia?

2. Summarize some of the early criticisms of the disease concept of schizophrenia. Evaluate them in light of more recent research.

3. Of the subtypes of schizophrenia, which are the most valid and likely to stand the test of time?

4. How consistent is the evidence linking dopamine activity to positive but not negative symptoms of schizophrenia?

5. Should the schizophrenia spectrum disorders really be classified in one group?

6. What is the prevalence of schizophrenia among the homeless?

7. Why is the onset of schizophrenia earlier among men than women?

8. What factors predict good outcome in schizophrenia?

9. Stress seems to contribute to schizophrenia. Is it possible to specify just what types of stress are crucial?

10. How might schizophrenia be prevented from developing in the first place?

11. What can be done to increase the participation of individuals with schizophrenia in aftercare programs?

12. How can clozapine be made more affordable?

13. Describe an integrated treatment of schizophrenia.

14. Evaluate Torrey's argument that schizophrenia may be caused by a virus (e.g., E. F. Torrey [1988]. Stalking the schizovirus. *Schizophrenia Bulletin, 14,* 223–229). If this proposal is correct, what are the implications for prevention and treatment of schizophrenia?

FURTHER READINGS

Arieti, S. (1974). *Interpretation of schizophrenia* (2nd ed.). New York: Basic Books.

Bateson, G., Jackson, D. D., Haley, J., & Weakland, J. (1956). Toward a theory of schizophrenia. *Behavioral Science, 1,* 251–264.

Bernheim, K. F., & Lewine, R. R. J. (1979). *Schizophrenia.* New York: Norton.

Bleuler, M. (1978). *The schizophrenic disorders: Long-term patient and family studies.* New Haven, CT: Yale University Press.

Crow, T. J. (1985). The two syndrome concept: Origins and current status. *Schizophrenia Bulletin, 11,* 471–486.

Fireside, H. (1979). *Soviet psychoprisons.* New York: Norton.

Goffman, E. (1961). *Asylums.* Garden City, NY: Anchor.

Gottesman, I. I. (1991). *Schizophrenia genesis: The origins of madness.* New York: Freeman.

Heinrichs, R. W. (1993). Schizophrenia and the brain: Conditions for a neuropsychology of madness. *American Psychologist, 48,* 221–233.

Laing, R. D. (1959). *The divided self.* London: Tavistok.

Mirsky, A. F., & Duncan, C. C. (1986). Etiology and expression of schizophrenia: Neurobiological and psychosocial factors. *Annual Review of Psychology, 37,* 291–319.

Rosenthal, D. (Ed.). (1963). *The Genain quadruplets.* New York: Basic Books.

Sarbin, T. R., & Mancuso, J. C. (1980). *Schizophrenia: Medical diagnosis or moral verdict?* New York: Pergamon.

Szasz, T. S. (1961). *The myth of mental illness.* New York: Hoeber.

Torrey, E. F. (1988). Stalking the schizovirus. *Schizophrenia Bulletin, 14,* 223–229.

Valenstein, E. S. (1986). *Great and desperate cures.* New York: Basic Books.

Wyatt, R. J., Alexander, R. C., Egan, M. F., & Kirch, D. G. (1988). Schizophrenia, just the facts: What do we know, how well do we know it? *Schizophrenia Research, 1,* 3–18.

CHAPTER 13

Personality Disorders

Maladaptive styles of behaving are described as personality disorders, which are covered in this chapter. After reading Chapter 13, you should be able to do the following:

- Understand why DSM-IV includes a category for personality disorders.
- Know why this diagnostic category is controversial.
- Define the specific personality disorders listed in DSM-IV.
- Compare and contrast these disorders with respect to symptoms, prevalence, epidemiology, causes, explanations, and treatments.
- Understand why certain personality disorders are not listed in DSM-IV.
- Appreciate how personality disorders can be conceived in dimensional terms.
- Explain why the idea of interactionism leads to a more satisfactory way of thinking about personality disorders.

CHAPTER SUMMARY

Introduction

Personality disorders are inflexible and maladaptive styles of behaving; they may exacerbate clinical syndromes as well as constitute problems in their own right. DSM-IV specifies 10 different personality disorders, and this particular list can be criticized both for what it includes and for what it does not.

Personality Typologies

Also subject to criticism is the DSM-IV assumption that people's personalities can be described in terms of discrete categories. Nonetheless, the general idea of a personality disorder adds something useful to our understanding of abnormality.

The Odd Personality Disorders

DSM-IV personality disorders fall into three groups. The first group consists of personality styles that can be characterized as odd. A person with a paranoid personality disorder displays a pervasive belief that other people intend to harm him. A person with a schizoid personality disorder shows widespread indifference to other people and a restricted range of emotional experience and expression. A person with a schizotypal personality disorder tends to be peculiar in thoughts, actions, and appearance.

The Dramatic Personality Disorders

The second group of DSM-IV personality disorders involves personality styles that are dramatic, emotional, and/or erratic. Those with antisocial personality disorder show long-standing patterns of behaving irresponsibly toward others. Borderline personality disorder refers to a style marked by instability in mood, relationships, and self-image. Histrionic personality disorder is an emotional and attention-seeking style. Those diagnosed with a narcissistic personality disorder are grandiose about the self, hypersensitive to what others think, and lacking in empathy.

The Timid Personality Disorders

The third group of DSM-IV personality disorders are marked by fearfulness and anxiety. Social discomfort, fear of evaluation, and timidity characterizes the avoidant personality disorder. An individual who is excessively dependent on and submissive to others has a dependent personality disorder. An obsessive-compulsive personality disorder refers to a perfectionistic and inflexible style of behaving.

Conclusions

In contrast to the DSM-IV approach, many contemporary theorists believe that problematic personality styles should be viewed on the one hand in terms of continuous dimensions of behaving and on the other hand in terms of their social context.

GLOSSARY TERMS

antisocial personality disorder—personality disorder involving a long-standing pattern of behaving irresponsibly to others

avoidant personality disorder—personality disorder involving widespread and long-standing social discomfort, fear of evaluation, and timidity

borderline personality disorder—personality disorder characterized by instability in mood, relationships, and self-image

dependent personality disorder—personality disorder in which the individual shows a widespread and long-standing pattern of being dependent on and submissive to others

histrionic personality disorder; hysterical personality disorder—personality disorder marked by excessive emotionality and attention-seeking

interactionism—the position that people's personality traits and their settings interact to determine what they do

narcissistic personality disorder—personality disorder characterized by a pervasive grandiosity about the self, hypersensitivity to what others think, and a lack of empathy

object relations—mental representations people have of themselves and others

obsessive-compulsive personality disorder—personality disorder characterized by perfectionism and inflexibility

paranoid personality disorder—personality disorder marked by the pervasive yet unwarranted belief that other people intend to do one harm

personality disorder—inflexible and maladaptive style of behaving

schizoid personality disorder—personality disorder marked by widespread indifference to other people and a restricted range of emotional experience and expression

schizotypal personality disorder—personality disorder characterized by peculiarities in thoughts, actions, and appearance

temperament—biologically based styles of behaving (e.g., a person's activity level)

NAMES AND DATES

Paul Meehl (1920–)

Narcissus

CONNECTIONS TO OTHER CHAPTERS

Personality disorders are an excellent example of the fuzzy boundaries of abnormality (Chapter 1). Not surprisingly, diagnostic reliability tends to be notably low for these disorders, and critics have suggested that maladaptive styles of behaving might better be viewed in dimensional terms (Chapter 2). Personality disorders have attracted attention over the years in part because they have been thought to predispose the sorts of clinical syndromes described in Chapters 5 through 12. This assumption is not widely supported by research, although the link between certain personality disorders and substance abuse (Chapter 5) on the one hand and schizophrenia (Chapter 12) on the other has been established.

The antisocial personality disorder diagnosis is one of the most reliable and valid described in DSM-IV. A biological basis (Chapter 6) has been implicated, which may lead to the low levels of anxiety (Chapter 7) experienced by many with this disorder. A biopsychosocial explanation (Chapter 3) seems viable for antisocial personality disorder and indeed may be preferable for all personality disorders.

Which maladaptive styles of behaving should be included in a diagnostic system? One safe prediction is that the 10 disorders catalogued in DSM-IV will not be listed indefinitely. Some may be viewed as variants of clinical syndromes. For example, perhaps avoidant personality disorder will be considered a type of anxiety disorder (Chapter 7), borderline personality disorder a type of dissociative disorder (Chapter 8) or mood disorder (Chapter 9), and schizotypal personality disorder a type of schizophrenia (Chapter 12). Newly identified personality disorders might be added. The lifestyles that contribute to organic disorders (Chapter 6) and mind-body disorders (Chapter 10) are likely candidates.

The origins of personality disorders in childhood (Chapter 14) are poorly understood. Also in need of further investigation are how best to treat these disorders and how to prevent them from developing in the first place (Chapter 3).

MULTIPLE-CHOICE QUESTIONS

1. Personality disorders are coded on _____ of DSM-IV.
    A. Axis I
    B. Axis II
    C. Axis III
    D. Axis IV
    E. Axis V

2. Personality disorders are included in DSM-IV because they:
    A. are problems in their own right
    B. presumably exacerbate clinical syndromes
    C. both A and B
    D. neither A nor B

3. According to clinical lore, those with personality disorders often respond _____ to psychotherapy.
    A. poorly
    B. sometimes poorly, sometimes well
    C. well

4. The specific personality disorders listed in DSM-IV can be criticized for what is:
    A. excluded
    B. included
    C. both A and B
    D. neither A nor B

5. DSM-IV conceptualizes personality disorders in terms of:
    A. a typology
    B. dimensions
    C. universal personality traits
    D. a combination of A and B

6. The personality disorder marked by unwarranted beliefs that someone else intends harm is _____ personality disorder.
   A. antisocial
   B. borderline
   C. paranoid
   D. schizoid
   E. schizotypal

7. Someone with paranoid personality disorder _____ psychotic.
   A. is
   B. is not

8. The personality disorder characterized by widespread indifference to others and restricted emotions is _____ personality disorder.
   A. antisocial
   B. borderline
   C. paranoid
   D. schizoid
   E. schizotypal

9. Anhedonia is a salient symptom of _____ personality disorder.
   A. antisocial
   B. borderline
   C. paranoid
   D. schizoid
   E. schizotypal

10. Those with _____ personality disorder are genetically related to individuals with schizophrenia.
    A. antisocial
    B. dependent
    C. narcissistic
    D. obsessive-compulsive
    E. schizotypal

11. The personality disorder characterized by peculiarity in thoughts, actions, and appearance is _____ personality disorder.
    A. antisocial
    B. borderline
    C. paranoid
    D. schizoid
    E. schizotypal

12. The personality disorder characterized by irresponsibility to others is _____ personality disorder.
    A. antisocial
    B. borderline
    C. paranoid
    D. schizoid
    E. schizotypal

13. The textbook cites Gary Gilmore as an example of someone with a(an) _____ personality disorder.
    A. antisocial
    B. borderline
    C. paranoid
    D. schizoid
    E. schizotypal

14. Research suggests that those with antisocial personality disorder are:
    A. chronically underaroused
    B. highly anxious
    C. mentally retarded
    D. psychotic
    E. severely depressed

15. Those with _____ personality disorder often have abnormal EEG patterns.
    A. antisocial
    B. avoidant
    C. borderline
    D. dependent
    E. narcissistic
    F. obsessive-compulsive

16. _____ personality disorder is characterized by marked instability.
    A. Antisocial
    B. Avoidant
    C. Borderline
    D. Dependent
    E. Narcissistic
    F. Obsessive-compulsive

17. Borderline personality disorder is frequently explained in terms of:
    A. faulty learning
    B. genetics
    C. low intelligence
    D. neurotransmitters
    E. object relations

18. _____ personality disorder is marked by excessive emotionality and attention-seeking.
    A. Antisocial
    B. Avoidant
    C. Borderline
    D. Histrionic
    E. Narcissistic
    F. Obsessive-compulsive

19. The personality disorder characterized by pervasive grandiosity and need for admiration is _____ personality disorder.
    A. antisocial
    B. avoidant
    C. borderline
    D. dependent
    E. narcissistic
    F. obsessive-compulsive

20. _____ theorists have long been interested in narcissistic personality disorder.
    A. Behavioral
    B. Biomedical
    C. Cognitive
    D. Family systems
    E. Psychodynamic

21. The personality disorder defined in terms of social discomfort, hypersensitivity to evaluation, and feelings of inadequacy is _____ personality disorder.
    A. antisocial
    B. avoidant
    C. borderline
    D. dependent
    E. narcissistic
    F. obsessive-compulsive

22. Timidity _____ heritable.
    A. is
    B. is not

23. _____ personality disorder is characterized by a widespread pattern of submissiveness to others.
    A. Antisocial
    B. Avoidant
    C. Borderline
    D. Dependent
    E. Narcissistic
    F. Obsessive-compulsive

24. Psychodynamic theorists interpret dependent personality disorder in terms of the defense mechanism of:
    A. denial
    B. displacement
    C. projection
    D. reaction formation
    E. sublimation

25. _____ personality disorder involves perfectionism and inflexibility.
    A. Antisocial
    B. Avoidant
    C. Borderline
    D. Dependent
    E. Histrionic
    F. Obsessive-compulsive

26. Obsessive-compulsive personality disorder _____ predispose obsessive-compulsive disorder.
    A. does
    B. does not

27. Personality disorders _____ in prevalence with age.
    A. decrease
    B. stay the same
    C. increase

28. Temperament is a style of behaving based in:
    A. biology
    B. classical conditioning
    C. modeling
    D. operant conditioning
    E. all of the above

29. In _____, the person unintentionally elicits a given response from the environment.
    A. evocation
    B. manipulation
    C. selection
    D. none of the above

30. In _____, the person intentionally alters the world.
    A. evocation
    B. manipulation
    C. selection
    D. none of the above

31. In _____, the person chooses to enter or avoid certain situations.
    A. evocation
    B. manipulation
    C. selection
    D. none of the above

32. Interactionism recognizes the joint influence of:
    A. emotion and cognition
    B. mind and body
    C. person and environment
    D. thought and deed

33. More common among males than females is _____ personality disorder.
    A. antisocial
    B. avoidant
    C. borderline
    D. dependent
    E. schizotypal

34. More common among females than males is _____ personality disorder.
    A. antisocial
    B. borderline
    C. paranoid
    D. schizoid
    E. schizotypal

Answers to Multiple-Choice Questions

1. B
2. C
3. A
4. C
5. A
6. C
7. B
8. D
9. D
10. E
11. E
12. A
13. A
14. A
15. A
16. C
17. E
18. D
19. E
20. E
21. B
22. A
23. D
24. D
25. F
26. B
27. A
28. A
29. A
30. B
31. C
32. C
33. A
34. B

Critical Thinking Questions and Research Paper Topics

1. Despite their lack of validity, why are personality typologies so compelling?

2. What styles of maladaptive behavior are left out of the DSM-IV list of personality disorders?

3. Starting from scratch, what styles of maladaptive behavior would you include in a list of personality disorders?

4. Think of "celebrity" examples of the DSM-IV personality disorders.

5. Of the personality disorders in DSM-IV, which seem to be the most valid?

6. Of the personality disorders in DSM-IV, which seem to be the least valid?

7. Are there cultural differences in the prevalence of personality disorders?

8. The "Big Five" approach to personality dimensions differentiates five separate personality traits. Can this description be expanded to include personality disorders? (See L. R. Goldberg [1993]. The structure of phenotypic personality traits. *American Psychologist, 48,* 26–34.)

9. Do personality disorders, no matter how they are defined, even belong in a diagnostic system?

10. Survey the evidence that personality disorders predispose clinical syndromes.

11. Why do personality disorders usually wane with age?

12. How might personality disorders be prevented from developing in the first place?

13. What are the childhood equivalents of adult personality disorders?

14. Are personality disorders inevitably interpersonal problems?

FURTHER READINGS

Beck, A. T., Freeman, A., & Associates. (1990). *Cognitive therapy of personality disorders.* New York: Guilford.

Bridgeman, H., & Drury, E. (Eds.). (1975). *The British eccentric.* London: Michael Joseph.

Buss, A. H., & Plomin, R. (1975). *A temperament theory of personality.* New York: Wiley.

Buss, A. H., & Plomin, R. (1984). *Temperament: Early developing personality traits.* Hillsdale, NJ: Erlbaum.

Buss, D. M. (1987). Selection, evocation, and manipulation. *Journal of Personality and Social Psychology, 53,* 1214–1221.

Cleckley, H. (1976). *The mask of sanity* (5th ed.). St. Louis: Mosby.

Freud, S. (1914). On narcissism. *Standard edition* (Vol. 14). London: Hogarth.

Greenberg, J. R., & Mitchell, S. A. (1983). *Object relations in psychoanalytic theory.* Cambridge: Harvard University Press.

Gunderson, J. G., & Singer, M. T. (1975). Defining borderline patients: An overview. *American Journal of Psychiatry, 132,* 1–10.

Lasch, C. (1978). *The culture of narcissism: American life in an age of diminishing expectations.* New York: Norton.

Mailer, N. (1979). *The executioner's song.* Boston: Little, Brown.

Meehl, P. E. (1990). Toward an integrated theory of schizotaxia, schizotypy, and schizophrenia. *Journal of Personality Disorders, 4,* 1–99.

Millon, T. (1990). *Toward a new personology.* New York: Wiley.

Rosewater, L. B. (1987). A critical analysis of the proposed self-defeating personality disorder. *Journal of Personality Disorders, 1,* 190–195.

Time-Life Books. (1992). *Odd and eccentric people.* Alexandria, VA: Author.

Tyrer, P. (Ed.). (1988). *Personality disorders: Diagnosis, management, and course.* London: Wright.

Walker, L. E. A. (1987). Inadequacies of the masochistic personality disorder diagnosis for women. *Journal of Personality Disorders, 1,* 183–189.

Weeks, D. J. (1988). *Eccentrics: The scientific investigation.* London: Stirling University Press.

Chapter 14

Disorders of Childhood and Adolescence

Psychology in general has recognized that people continue to change throughout their life span. Generalizations need to be qualified by specifying the appropriate developmental context. Applied to abnormality, this means that people's problems are defined, explained, and treated in terms of where they occur in development. This chapter covers the common psychological problems of children and adolescents. After reading this chapter, you should be able to do the following:

- Explain why the problems of children and adolescents can be particularly difficult to understand.
- Compare and contrast such disorders as mental retardation, learning difficulties, autism, attention-deficit/hyperactivity disorder, conduct disorder, separation anxiety disorder, and eating disorders with respect to symptoms, prevalence, epidemiology, causes, explanations, and treatments.
- Appreciate that all disorders have a developmental trajectory.

Chapter Summary

Introduction

The psychology of abnormality increasingly recognizes that people's problems should be described in the context of development, specifying where people find themselves in the life course. This recognition is in keeping with the larger trend in developmental psychology of specifying an ever finer division of the life span. To date, this developmental perspective has been brought to bear most fully on the particular problems of children and adolescents, and these are the focus of this chapter.

Mental Retardation

Mental retardation refers to a problem first evident during childhood in which an individual displays below average intellectual functioning and an impaired ability to meet the demands of everyday life. In organic retardation, the problem is clearly linked to a specific illness, injury, or physiological abnormality. For example, if pregnant women use alcohol or drugs, this may result in mental retardation among their offspring. Down syndrome is another form of organic retardation, in this case caused by an extra set of genes. In sociocultural retardation, the problem is not linked to a biological cause; it is instead considered the result of social disadvantage.

The psychological mechanisms of mental retardation include difficulties with attention, short-term memory, rapid information processing, and meta-cognition. Treatment of mental retardation involves prevention when possible and remediation through specific instruction.

Learning Difficulties

Learning difficulties are circumscribed problems with acquiring or performing a specific skill such as reading or speaking. Explanations run from neurological abnormalities to socialization.

Autism

Autism is a profound disturbance in social interaction and communication, apparently due to biological causes, perhaps abnormally high levels of serotonin. Medication and behavior therapy are currently popular treatments of autism. In general, though, prognosis is poor.

Attention-Deficit/Hyperactivity Disorder

Children with attention-deficit/hyperactivity disorder (ADHD) display a high activity level coupled with an inability to sustain attention. The causes of ADHD are not clear, but hypotheses have suggested neurological problems, environmental toxins, and social disadvantage. Some children with ADHD can be helped with stimulants.

Conduct Disorder

Conduct disorder is marked by a child's consistent violation of the rights of others. It appears to be a forerunner of antisocial personality disorder among adults and is explained in much the same way: by a combination of biological and social influences. In some cases, conduct disorder can be alleviated through behavior therapy, but the most severe forms often prove intractable.

Separation Anxiety Disorder

Children may experience the same fear and anxiety disorders encountered among adults, but DSM-IV additionally specifies a problem unique to children: separation anxiety disorder. Cognitive-behavioral techniques appear to be the most useful treatment.

Eating Disorders

Obesity is the accumulation of excess body fat. Quite common in the United States today, obesity has numerous causes, several of which date to childhood. Obesity is relatively easy to treat in the short run, yet quite difficult to treat in the long run.

Anorexia is the refusal to maintain a minimal body weight. Most common among adolescent females, this disorder may be fatal in as many as 21% of the cases. Its causes are the subject of debate, and consistently effective treatments have not yet been devised. Currently favored strategies are family therapy and behavior therapy.

In bulimia, an individual ingests large amounts of high-calorie food and then rids herself of it, often through vomiting. Bulimia is most common among young adult females, and it usually co-occurs with depression. The causes of bulimia are as poorly understood as those of anorexia. Antidepressant medication, behavior therapy, and cognitive therapy are currently popular treatments.

GLOSSARY TERMS

anorexia nervosa—eating disorder characterized by refusal to maintain minimal body weight

attention-deficit/hyperactivity disorder; ADHD—disorder marked by high activity level and inability to pay attention

autism; autistic disorder—pervasive developmental disorder characterized by gross impairment in social interaction and communication

bulimia nervosa—eating disorder that involves ingesting large amounts of high-calorie food in a short amount of time, feeling out of control while doing so, and then ridding oneself of these calories

cohort differences—psychological differences among groups of people born at different times and places

conduct disorder—disorder in which a child is socially disruptive and upsetting to others

crack baby—baby born to a mother addicted to crack cocaine

developmental psychopathology—the field that studies disorders in their developmental context

Dexedrine—stimulant used to treat ADHD

Down syndrome—common form of organic retardation, caused by the presence of an extra set of genes on the 21st chromosome

echolalia—symptom of autism: echoing back whatever is said, rather than responding to it

fenfluramine—an amphetamine that reduces the level of serotonin in the blood, used as a treatment for autism

fetal alcohol syndrome—complex of characteristics seen among children born to alcoholic mothers: small size, heart and limb defects, distinctive facial features, and mental retardation

intelligence quotient; IQ—numerical estimate of intelligence derived from an intelligence test; traditionally, the quotient of mental age to chronological age, multiplied by 100

learning disorders—difficulties encountered with acquiring or performing a specific skill relevant to reading, writing, and arithmetic

mainstreaming—the practice of educating those with mental retardation in the same schools as other children and often in the same classrooms

mental retardation—problem first evident during childhood in which an individual displays below average intellectual functioning and impaired ability to meet demands of everyday life

minimal brain damage; MBD—subtle neurological damage once thought to be the cause of learning disorders

obesity—excess accumulation of body fat, conventionally defined as some percentage—like 20%—in excess weight over what is considered average for a person of a given sex, age, and height

organic retardation—mental retardation clearly linked to a specific illness, injury, or physiological abnormality

pronominal reversal—symptom of autism: substituting *you* for *I*

Ritalin—stimulant used to treat ADHD

separation anxiety disorder—anxiety disorder of childhood characterized by excessive anxiety about being separated from a caretaker (e.g., parent) and/or familiar surroundings

serotonin—a neurotransmitter hypothesized to be involved in some cases of autism

sociocultural retardation—mental retardation that cannot be traced specifically to physical causes

NAMES AND DATES

Alfred Binet (1857–1911)

Leo Kanner (1894–1981)

CONNECTIONS TO OTHER CHAPTERS

As noted in Chapter 14, psychologists have recently recognized that there are few invariants across the life span. The familiar models of abnormality (Chapter 3) cannot be glibly generalized from adults to children, and matters of assessment (Chapter 2) and even the very definition of abnormality (Chapter 1) must be qualified by statements about developmental stages. Treatments, of course, take different forms depending on where the individual happens to be in the life course (Chapter 3).

This developmental perspective to date has been most fully applied to the problems of children and adolescents, although good efforts are also being made with respect to problems common among the elderly, such as organic disorders (Chapter 6) and mind-body disorders (Chapter 10). The irony is that our understanding of the problems of "generic" adults (Chapters 5–13) now lags behind recent efforts to understand segments of the population relatively neglected in the past.

Some problems have similarities across the life span, such as anxiety disorders (Chapter 7) and depression (Chapter 9). Others manifest themselves differently, such as schizophrenia (Chapter 12). In any event, most agree that problems have a developmental trajectory, meaning that early experiences and events often influence what follows, for better or worse. This explains why so many attempts at primary prevention of problems (Chapter 3) target children.

Like the field of developmental psychopathology, the judicial system recognizes that children cannot be treated like miniature adults. Many of the generalizations about our legal system and how it interacts with abnormal psychology (Chapter 15) must similarly be qualified by taking into account whether the individuals in question are children or adults.

MULTIPLE-CHOICE QUESTIONS

1. A cohort difference refers to a difference among:
    A. individuals with many friends versus those with few friends
    B. males and females
    C. people born during different historical periods
    D. people of different ages
    E. those of different cultures

142 Chapter 14

2. Mental retardation is usually defined as:
   A. impaired adaptation
   B. low intelligence
   C. both A and B
   D. neither A nor B

3. Modern intelligence tests were developed by:
   A. Binet
   B. Erikson
   C. Freud
   D. Hall
   E. Watson

4. The two major types of mental retardation are:
   A. chronic and acute
   B. male and female
   C. mild and severe
   D. organic and sociocultural
   E. treatable and untreatable

5. Mental retardation occurs more frequently among:
   A. females
   B. males
   C. females and males equally

6. Down syndrome is caused by a problem with:
   A. chromosomes
   B. dependency
   C. learning
   D. parenting
   E. protein metabolism

7. Mainstreaming refers to the:
   A. assumption that learning disabilities will be outgrown
   B. biomedical treatment of conduct disorder
   C. education of retarded children with nonretarded children
   D. importance of the family for normal development
   E. necessity to offer conclusions about learning disabilities separately for females and males

8. Learning disabilities are diagnosed among _____ of contemporary United States children.
   A. 1%
   B. 5%
   C. 10%
   D. 25%
   E. 40%

9. Learning disabilities occur more frequently among:
   A. females
   B. males
   C. females and males equally

10. When first described, autism was interpreted in _____ terms; now it is interpreted in _____ terms.
    A. biological; biological
    B. biological; psychological
    C. psychological; biological
    D. psychological; psychological

11. Fenfluramine, a drug used to treat autism, is a(n):
    A. amphetamine
    B. antidepressant
    C. major tranquilizer
    D. minor tranquilizer
    E. steroid

12. Attention-deficit/hyperactivity disorder overlaps considerably with:
    A. childhood schizophrenia
    B. conduct disorder
    C. mental retardation
    D. obesity
    E. separation anxiety disorder

13. The biomedical treatment of attention-deficit/hyperactivity disorder is:
    A. Depo-Provera
    B. Ritalin
    C. Thorazine
    D. Valium

14. Conduct disorder in children frequently foreshadows _____ in adults.
    A. antisocial personality disorder
    B. bipolar disorder
    C. obsessive-compulsive disorder
    D. schizophrenia
    E. transvestism

15. An emotional bond between infant and caretaker typically occurs in the infant's _____ year of life.
    A. first
    B. second
    C. third
    D. fourth
    E. fifth

16. Obesity is conventionally defined as _____ in excess of normal weight.
    A. 5%
    B. 10%
    C. 20%
    D. 50%
    E. 75%

17. Adopted children resemble their _____ parents with respect to weight.
    A. adoptive
    B. biological
    C. both A and B
    D. neither A nor B

18. In 40% of the cases of anorexia, cessation of menstruation _____ weight loss.
    A. precedes
    B. accompanies
    C. follows

19. Weight loss strategies usually work in the _____ run, not in the _____ run.
    A. long; short
    B. short; long

20. The causes of anorexia are generally agreed to be:
    A. biological
    B. environmental
    C. neither A nor B
    D. both A and B
    E. no causes are agreed upon

21. Psychodynamic theorists explain anorexia in terms of conflicts about:
    A. independence
    B. maturity
    C. sexuality
    D. all of the above
    E. none of the above

22. _____ is more likely to be fatal.
    A. Anorexia
    B. Bulimia
    C. anorexia and bulimia are equally fatal

23. Bulimia frequently co-occurs with:
    A. anxiety
    B. asthma
    C. depression
    D. schizophrenia
    E. substance abuse

24. Developmental psychopathologists usually adhere to a _____ model of abnormality.
    A. biomedical
    B. biopsychosocial
    C. cognitive-behavioral
    D. family systems
    E. psychoanalytic

25. A child with brain damage is likely to make a(n) _____ satisfactory recovery than (as) an adult with a similar injury.
    A. less
    B. equally
    C. more

26. Unipolar disorder among children tends to be characterized chiefly by _____ symptoms.
    A. behavioral
    B. cognitive
    C. emotional
    D. physiological

27. Schizophrenia among children, as compared with adults, is _____ likely to be characterized by hallucinations and delusions.
    A. less
    B. equally
    C. more

Answers to Multiple-Choice Questions

1. C
2. C
3. A
4. D
5. B
6. A
7. C
8. C
9. B
10. C
11. A
12. B
13. C
14. A
15. A
16. C
17. B
18. A
19. B
20. E
21. D
22. A
23. C
24. B
25. C
26. C
27. A

Critical Thinking Questions and Research Paper Topics

1. What are the characteristic disorders of early, middle, and later adulthood?

2. Erik Erikson argues that in the course of life, people must resolve several psychosocial issues. What psychological problems result from failure to resolve these issues? (See E. H. Erikson [1963]. *Childhood and society* [2nd ed.]. New York: Norton.)

3. Why do so many different psychological disorders have their onset during adolescence?

4. How might a diagnostic interview with a young child best be conducted?

5. Describe how mental retardation might be prevented from developing in the first place.

6. What are the pros and cons of mainstreaming?

7. Do learning disabilities belong in a diagnostic system, or are they better regarded as educational problems?

8. Why was autism not described before the 1940s?

9. Attention-deficit/hyperactivity disorder and conduct disorder frequently co-occur. Can we say which is primary?

10. There are apparently ethnic differences in attention-deficit/hyperactivity disorder. What are they? Why do they exist?

11. Many of the childhood and adolescent disorders are more prevalent among males than females. Discuss this sex difference. What do the exceptions tell us?

12. How do the various anxiety disorders manifest themselves in young children?

13. How does unipolar depression manifest itself in young children?

14. What can be done to prevent obesity from developing in the first place?

15. Should anorexia and bulimia be classified together as versions of the same disorder, or are they distinct?

FURTHER READINGS

Achenbach, T. M. (1985). *Assessment and taxonomy of child and adolescent psychopathology.* Newbury Park, CA: Sage.

Aries, P. (1962). *Centuries of childhood: A social history of family life.* New York: Vintage.

Bell, R. M. (1985). *Holy anorexia.* Chicago: University of Chicago Press.

Bettelheim, B. (1967). *The empty fortress.* New York: Free Press.

Brownell, K. D., & Wadden, T. A. (1992). Etiology and treatment of obesity: Understanding a serious, prevalent, and refractory disorder. *Journal of Consulting and Clinical Psychology, 60,* 505–517.

Bruch, H. (1978). *The golden cage: The enigma of anorexia nervosa.* Cambridge: Harvard University Press.

Edgerton, R. E. (1979). *Mental retardation.* Cambridge: Harvard University Press.

Feingold, B. F. (1976). Hyperkinesis and learning disabilities linked to the ingestion of artificial food colors and flavors. *Journal of Learning Disabilities, 9,* 551–559.

Gardner, H. (1983). *Frames of mind: The theory of multiple intelligences.* New York: Basic Books.

Gould, S. J. (1981). *The mismeasure of man.* New York: Norton.

Herrnstein, R. J., & Murray, C. (1994). *The bell curve: Intelligence and class structure in American life.* New York: Free Press.

Kanner, L. (1943). Autistic disturbances of affective contact. *Nervous Child, 2,* 217–250.

Minuchin, S., Rosman, B. L., & Baker, L. (1978). *Psychosomatic families.* Cambridge: Harvard University Press.

Ollendick, T. H., & Hersen, M. (Eds.). (1989). *Handbook of child psychopathology* (2nd ed.). New York: Plenum.

Schotte, D., & Stunkard, A. J. (1987). Bulimia vs bulimic behaviors on a college campus. *JAMA, 258,* 1213–1215.

Treffert, D. A. (1989). *Extraordinary people: Understanding "idiot savants."* New York: Harper & Row.

Chapter 15

Abnormality in a Community and Legal Context

This final chapter discusses two aspects of the social context of abnormal psychology: the community mental health movement and the legal system. After reading this chapter, you should be able to do the following:

- Sketch the history of the community mental health movement in the United States.
- Describe the role of the American Psychological Association in overseeing professional activities of psychologists.
- Understand how psychologists function as expert witnesses in court cases.
- Specify the rights of those with psychological disorders.
- Understand the intent of the insanity plea.
- Compare and contrast different criteria for determining insanity.
- Describe the concepts of competence to stand trial and competence to be punished.

Chapter Summary

The Community Mental Health Movement

In the United States, prevention has been linked with the community mental health movement, which began with great expectations in the 1960s. One of the goals of the community mental health movement was to shift the care of people with psychological problems from large state hospitals to smaller clinics in the community. More profoundly, community mental health centers were charged as well with preventing problems from occurring in the first place.

Although the number of patients in psychiatric hospitals decreased dramatically in the 1970s and 1980s, the number of homeless individuals with psychological problems increased. In other words, community mental health centers did not take over the responsibility of caring for these people from state psychiatric hospitals. The important goal of prevention was largely neglected by the community mental health movement.

In recent years, this movement has been moribund. The reasons are subject to debate. Some point to insufficient federal funding, others to the less than efficient way that many community mental health centers were run.

Psychology as a Profession

The American Psychological Association is a national organization that tries to promote psychology as a profession. To this end, it maintains a code of conduct, evaluates graduate training programs and internships, and takes public stances on issues affecting psychology.

Psychologists as Expert Witnesses

Although psychology and the judicial system have frequent contact, they embody different ways of understanding human conduct. Psychology assumes that behavior has causes and attempts to offer generalizations about people per se. The legal system, in contrast, assumes that behavior is freely chosen unless there exist extenuating circumstances, and attempts to render decisions about individual persons.

The Rights of Those with Disorders

About 25% of admissions to psychiatric hospitals are involuntary, carried out over the individual's objections. The process of involuntary commitment is done under the supervision of the legal system. It requires that an individual be judged dangerous to the self and/or others. These judgments are far from foolproof, and involuntary commitment is thus controversial.

In recent decades, various rights of psychiatric patients have been recognized. Individuals in hospitals are guaranteed such civil rights as voting and making a will. They have the right to receive treatment as well as the right to refuse it. And they are entitled to the least restrictive environment that can be provided. However, these rights can be abridged if exercising them is thought to work against the patient's good.

What clients tell their therapists is confidential, except when it involves child abuse or specific threats against another person. Then the therapist is required to break confidentiality.

Abnormality and Crime

A person with a psychological problem who is accused of a crime may plead not guilty by reason of insanity. Insanity is a legal term, not a psychological one, and different criteria for judging insanity have been proposed. Despite the great interest that the insanity plea stimulates, it occurs in only a small fraction of criminal cases.

Much more common is a person being deemed incompetent to stand trial because of a current psychological problem that makes it impossible for him or her to understand or participate in legal proceedings. Most individuals judged incompetent eventually stand trial.

A person may also be judged incompetent to be punished, which means that by virtue of a psychological problem, he or she does not understand the sentence given. Instead of being sent away to a prison, the person instead goes to a forensic hospital for treatment; the distinction may exist more in principle than in practice.

Glossary Terms

American Law Institute rule; ALI rule—a rule for judging an insanity plea: Did the crime in question result from a mental disease or defect of the person so that he lacked substantial capacity either to appreciate the wrongfulness of his conduct or to conform his conduct to the requirements of law?

competent to stand trial—the judgment that an individual can understand legal proceedings and contribute to his or her own defense

determinism—philosophical assumption that what people do has causes

Durham rule—a rule for judging an insanity plea: Did the crime in question result from the person's mental disease or mental defect?

duty to warn—therapist's obligation to warn people that a client has made specific threats against their life

free will—philosophical assumption that what people do represents their own choice

guilty but mentally ill verdict; GBMI verdict—a controversial court verdict that allows a person to be judged both insane and guilty of a crime

insanity plea—defense against an accusation on the grounds that the individual suffered from a psychological problem at the time the crime was committed

involuntary commitment—admission to a psychiatric hospital against an individual's will

M'Naghten rule—a rule for judging an insanity plea: At the time of the crime, did the person suffer from a problem so that he did not know what he was doing or did not know that what he was doing was wrong?

partial hospitalization—provision of care to a person who does not need round-the-clock hospitalization, yet needs more care than weekly or monthly visits to a therapist

thank-you test—a suggested criterion for involuntary commitment: Will the involuntarily committed individual, once recovered from whatever problem he or she suffers, thank those who carried out the commitment?

therapeutic community—treatment strategy in which hospital patients live together in democratic fashion and work with staff members to regulate their own behavior, privileges, and eventual discharge

Names and Dates

American Psychological Association (founded 1892)

James Carter (1924–)

Community Mental Health Centers Act (passed 1963)

John F. Kennedy (1917–1963)

National Institute of Mental Health (founded 1946)

Know the history of the community mental health movement, as well as the history of the insanity plea, and how different criteria for insanity were proposed in response to earlier rules.

CONNECTIONS TO OTHER CHAPTERS

The community mental health movement has been the most ambitious attempt in the United States to prevent or minimize psychological disorders (Chapters 5–14). It reminds us that disorders exist in a social context.

Psychology's links with the legal system are but one more example of the need to contextualize a field by specifying the societal and historical influences upon it. In this case, the interaction between psychology and law is not always an easy one because their different underlying assumptions may clash. Among psychologists, only the humanistic-existential-phenomenological theorists have much to say about free will (Chapter 3), yet the legal system is fundamentally based on the premise that people freely undertake their actions.

Continued discussion of when people should or should not be held responsible for what they do might clarify how we think about certain psychological problems to which behavior contributes, such as substance abuse (Chapter 5), organic disorders (Chapter 6), mind-body disorders (Chapter 10), and eating disorders (Chapter 14). There is a tendency among some of us to blame people who suffer problems like these, but this may not always be reasonable or fair (Chapter 3).

Many of the ways in which psychology and the judicial system interact have to do with patients in apparent need of treatment (Chapter 3). Rights and responsibilities on both sides of the therapist-client relationship have been articulated. Legal notions like involuntary commitment and insanity have changed throughout the years and are still doing so. Here, at least, is a parallel with the science of psychology, which also finds itself in constant flux (Chapter 2).

MULTIPLE-CHOICE QUESTIONS

1. The community mental health movement was begun because of:
    A. discontent with traditional mental health services
    B. scientific breakthroughs in the community treatment of problems
    C. the availability of excess federal money following World War II
    D. the example provided by a similar movement in Canada

2. The National Institute of Mental Health was founded in:
    A. 1776
    B. 1861
    C. 1918
    D. 1946
    E. 1963

3. The Community Mental Health Centers Act was signed into law by President:
    A. Eisenhower
    B. Johnson
    C. Kennedy
    D. Nixon
    E. Roosevelt
    F. Truman

4. The goal of prevention inherent in the community mental health movement _____ met.
   A. was
   B. was not

5. According to the American Psychological Association's code of ethics, psychologists:
   A. are aware of their responsibility to the community and society in which they work and live
   B. contribute to the welfare of those with whom they interact professionally
   C. seek to promote integrity in their science, teaching, and practice
   D. all of the above
   E. none of the above

6. Psychology assumes _____, and the legal system assumes _____.
   A. determinism; determinism
   B. determinism; free will
   C. free will; determinism
   D. free will; free will

7. Psychology is concerned with _____, and the legal system is concerned with _____.
   A. generalizations about people; generalizations about people
   B. generalizations about people; individual persons
   C. individual persons; generalizations about people
   D. individual persons; individual persons

8. Under current law, involuntary commitment _____ last indefinitely without review.
   A. can
   B. cannot

9. Involuntary commitment can be undertaken when a person poses a danger to:
   A. self
   B. others
   C. both A and B
   D. either A or B
   E. neither A nor B

10. When involuntary commitment is actually undertaken, it is usually because the person poses a danger to:
    A. self
    B. others
    C. both A and B
    D. neither A nor B

11. Research suggests that psychologists _____ predict dangerousness.
    A. can
    B. cannot

12. Which of these rights are guaranteed to mental patients?
    A. the right to receive treatment
    B. the right to the least restrictive environment possible
    C. the right to vote
    D. all of the above
    E. none of the above

13. A therapist must break confidentiality in cases of:
    A. any suspected crime
    B. psychosis
    C. substance abuse
    D. suspected child abuse
    E. none of the above

14. A therapist has the duty to warn in the case of:
    A. any and all threats
    B. repeated threats
    C. serious threats
    D. threats against a specific person

15. When the insanity plea is offered in the United States, the crime in question is usually:
    A. assault
    B. homicide
    C. rape
    D. robbery

16. Under the _____ rule, insanity involves failure at the time of the crime to know what was done or that it was wrong.
    A. American Law Institute
    B. Durham
    C. M'Naghten
    D. all of the above
    E. none of the above

17. Under the _____ rule, an insanity ruling requires that the crime results from a mental disease or defect.
    A. American Law Institute
    B. Durham
    C. M'Naghten
    D. all of the above
    E. none of the above

18. The most stringent insanity criteria are contained in the _____ rule.
    A. American Law Institute
    B. Durham
    C. M'Naghten

19. The most flexible insanity criteria are contained in the _____ rule.
    A. American Law Institute
    B. Durham
    C. M'Naghten

20. The textbook describes the guilty but mentally ill verdict as:
    A. a contradiction in terms
    B. an improvement over other possible verdicts
    C. emotionally appealing
    D. both A and B
    E. both A and C
    F. both B and C

21. Can a psychologist testify in court about a research study he or she did *not* personally conduct?
    A. no
    B. yes

22. In many court cases involving children, the best interests of the _____ take precedence.
    A. child
    B. parent
    C. society

Answers to Multiple-Choice Questions

1. A
2. D
3. C
4. B
5. D
6. B
7. B
8. B
9. D
10. B
11. B
12. D
13. D
14. D
15. B
16. C
17. B
18. C
19. A
20. E
21. B
22. A

Critical Thinking Questions and Research Paper Topics

1. Trace changes over the past few decades in federal funding priorities for community mental health.

2. In the late 1980s, a rival organization to the American Psychological Association (APA) was founded: the American Psychological Society (APS). What were the reasons for the creation of a new organization to represent psychology as a profession?

3. Why are psychologists frequently political liberals?

4. Some argue that psychologists have no special knowledge that qualifies them to be expert witnesses in court cases. Do you agree? (See L. Coleman [1984]. *The reign of error: Psychiatry, authority, and law.* Boston: Beacon.)

5. What special considerations are involved when children testify (as victims) in child abuse cases?

6. Compare and contrast involuntary commitment procedures in different countries.

7. Review the research on the "dangerousness" of schizophrenic patients. What kinds of crimes do they typically commit?

8. Why are lower-class males overrepresented among those who are involuntarily committed?

9. Hospitalized patients are not guaranteed effective treatment, but should they be told this explicitly? Would this disclaimer undercut the effectiveness of treatment?

10. Describe the pros and cons of using physical restraints with mental patients who are out of control. Compare physical restraints with chemical restraints (e.g., major tranquilizers). Which is more humane?

11. Compare and contrast the use of the insanity plea across different nations.

12. Compare and contrast the use of the insanity plea across different states in the United States.

13. Compare and contrast forensic hospitals to prisons on the one hand and to psychiatric hospitals on the other.

FURTHER READINGS

Bloom, B. L. (1984). *Community mental health: A general introduction* (2nd ed.). Monterey, CA: Brooks/Cole.

Brodsky, S. L. (1991). *Testifying in court: Guidelines and maxims for the expert witness.* Washington, DC: American Psychological Association.

Caplan, L. (1984). *The insanity defense and the trial of John W. Hinckley, Jr.* Boston: Godine.

Coleman, L. (1984). *The reign of error: Psychiatry, authority, and law.* Boston: Beacon.

Guyer, M. J. (1990). Child psychiatry and legal liability: Implications of recent case law. *Journal of the American Academy of Child and Adolescent Psychiatry, 29,* 958–962.

Hilgard, E. R. (1987). *Psychology in America: A historical survey.* San Diego: Harcourt Brace Jovanovich.

Hornblower, M. (1987, November 23). Down and out—but determined. Does a mentally disturbed woman have the right to be homeless? *Time,* p. 29.

Klerman, G. L. (1990). The psychiatric patient's right to effective treatment: Implications of Osheroff v. Chestnut Lodge. *American Journal of Psychiatry, 147,* 409–418.

Lindsey, K. P., & Paul, G. L. (1989). Involuntary commitments to public mental health institutions: Issues involving the overrepresentation of blacks and assessment of relevant functioning. *Psychological Bulletin, 106,* 171–183.

Loftus, E. F. (1993). The reality of repressed memories. *American Psychologist, 48,* 518–537.

Loftus, E. F., & Monahan, J. (1980). Trial by data: Psychological research as legal evidence. *American Psychologist, 35,* 270–283.

Monahan, J., & Walker, L. (1988). Social science research in law: A new paradigm. *American Psychologist, 43,* 465–472.

Morris, N. (1982). *Madness and the criminal law.* Chicago: University of Chicago Press.

Szasz, T. S. (1963). *Law, liberty, and psychiatry: An inquiry into the social uses of mental health practices.* New York: Macmillan.